Street Life

Other Books by the Authors

Rob Lacey
the street bible
the essential street bible CD

Nick Page
The Bible Book
Blue
The Church Invisible

street life

engaging 40 big issues with the street bible

rob lacey & nick page

GRAND RAPIDS, MICHIGAN 49530 USA

We want to hear from you. Please send your comments about this book to us in care of zreview@zondervan.com. Thank you.

ZONDERVAN™

street life

Requests for information should be addressed to:

Zondervan, *Grand Rapids, Michigan 49530*

ISBN 0-310-25739-5

The website addresses recommended throughout this book are offered as a resource to you. These websites are not intended in any way to be or imply an endorsement on the part of Zondervan, nor do we vouch for their content for the life of this book.

Interior design by Beth Shagene

Printed in the United Kingdom

04 05 06 07 08 09 10 /❖ CLY/ 10 9 8 7 6 5 4 3 2 1

CONTENTS

HOW TO USE THIS BOOK

street life

Sets the scene. A situation, a picture, a mental image from everyday life. Imagine yourself walking along your very own high street. Just a bit of fiction/humour from an imaginary character to get the topic on its way.

street bible

Excerpts from *the street bible.* Some bits from the book that's out already; some bits that are brand new. The Bible is what this book is all about, so don't just read *the street bible* bits – go ahead and look it up in a proper translation. And why should you listen to the Bible anyway? Here are some clues:

Hebrews 4:12-16

'Cos God's Instruction Manual is vivid, vibrant, action-packed with spiritual muscle, it penetrates deeper than a Kalashnikov bullet – it gets between body and soul, gets right into your joints, your bone marrow. It susses out who's behind all your fronts. Nothing in the cosmos can hide from God. It all comes up on his monitor screens. Everything is digitally recorded, zoomed in on, watched and remembered by God's photographic memory. And we've got to stand there and explain it all in front of him!! There'll be no bluffing.

2 Timothy 3:15-17

Paul writes to Timothy . . .

You know where your coaching comes from – you've had the Instruction Manual since you were a toddler, and it's oozing wisdom. It sorts you out when you take the Liberator, Jesus, at his word. It's all straight from God's mouth, totally inspired. It's the only manual you need for coaching, counselling, correcting. If you want to be up and ready for every possible variation on Doing the Right Thing, then the Instruction Manual is the only book for you.

street wise

Reflections on the Bible passages. A look at life in the light of the Bible. Stuff to make you think, make you smile, even make you irritated. Certainly, stuff to learn. More important, stuff to do. See, that's the difference with the Bible: reading it might mean doing it; learning about it might mean living it. Christianity is all about real life. It's not a set of ideas to just sit and ponder about while fiddling with your navel ring. It's not a bundle of beliefs that we hide away inside our heads. No, it's a faith that we have to relate to real life. We have to make the words mean something, make them count.

And when it comes to the Bible, even though the words were written thousands of years back, they wrestle with the same issues that are giving us grief. People might have had different customs, walked down different streets, worn different brands of trainers, but they still had to grapple with the same problems we do: jealousy, envy, failure, joy, love, lust, anxiety – the same stuff that fills our lives filled their lives. And the same God was there to help them deal with it.

The thing is that the stuff all around us contains messages from God . . . if we're tuned in. The streets of earth contain shortcuts to the streets of heaven. What we do down here has a divine perspective and everyone we meet has the potential to love God and live forever with him. Ladders and lip gloss, sex shops and smog, beggars, bin men and bus-stops – they're all launching points for learning something about the way God sees things.

streetlights

More for you to explore from the proper Bible. Get yourself a good modern translation (not a paraphrase), look up the streetlights passages and explore what the Big Book itself has to say. Get a broader picture of what God says throughout his bestseller, not just a 'snapshot,' which might not tell the whole story (some horrific theories have been launched from one or two Bible verses taken out of context – ask Nelson Mandela).

For starters, read Psalm 119 – yes, all of it, but especially v. 105 – 'Your word is a lamp to my feet and a light for my path' . . . (Guess where we got the 'streetlights' title from!)

signposts

Voices from some of the Urban Heroes who have walked the streets before us.

Quotes to make you sit up and take notice.

Something to get you started:

Belief is a truth held in the mind.
Faith is a fire in the heart.
–Joseph Newton

To expect God to do everything while we do nothing is not faith, but superstition.
–Martin Luther King Jr

We must not only pause to reflect upon passages from the Bible, but upon 'slices of life', too, relating them together, and to the will of the Risen Christ for us.
–Michel Quoist

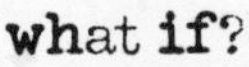

what if?

Asking questions about the Bible, about our faith, about God, is not a bad thing. (The Bible is full of people who asked, 'What if?' Some even risked the 'Why?' question.) These are just a few questions to start you off in your exploration of the topic; a few things to think about as you see what the Bible has to say. Use these, use your own questions, but whatever you do, think:

Something to get you started:

What if Christians really were different?

What if our lifestyle brought heaven on earth?

Is it possible to live God's way in God's world?

Who won the FA Cup in 1927?*

*Cardiff City, 1–0 against the Arsenal.

straight ahead!

Hey, radical! Take the action points and . . . well, uh . . . put them into action. Things you can do as a response. Of course, you'll come up with your own ideas and plans as well.

Something to get you started:

Don't just read *the street bible,* look up the verses in a proper Bible – one with a capital 'B'!

Tell your pastor/vicar/minister/priest/youth leader, 'I want to do something that'll make a difference, bring heaven on earth.' Time their response!

Surf the web for charities you could get stuck into helping.

Get your house group to use this book. Get your house group to buy twenty copies of this book . . . each. Cut out the middleman and just send Rob and Nick your money, jewels, gold ingots, exotic spices, Nubian slaves, etc., etc. . . .

way out!

Your handy get-out clause. Don't like what you're reading? This bit contains all you need to make a quick getaway.

Something to stop you starting:

Ask for your money back.

Use this product's absorbent qualities around the kitchen.

Begin an urban myth about either of this book's authors to totally discredit them in the public eye. (Not that it will take much.)

Ask your aunt to give you socks for your birthday next time.

Get yourself another, less demanding religion!

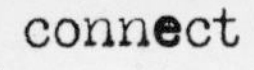

These one-word prayers are not meant to be the only communication between you and God. Who are we to tell you what to say? It's private. Just you and him. But we're happy to jump-start you with a provocative word, and then leave you to see what happens in the dot-dot-dot bits. Feel free to say 'Absolutely!' or 'Not 'arf' if 'Amen' has no meaning to you any more.

Something to get you started:

'O Lord, *oy!* . . . Amen.'

taking it further

Although we suggest a lot of ideas to help you think about these topics and put things into action, here are a few ideas that you can apply to *all* the topics in this book.

ask questions

I keep six honest serving-men
(They taught me all I knew);
Their names are What and Why and When
And How and Where and Who.
–Rudyard Kipling

When you read the Bible ask yourself these questions.

- **What**'s happening in the passage? What's the big idea behind this passage? What style is the writing? Is its teaching meant to be taken literally, or poetry meant to be interpreted more laterally?
- **Why** is this passage important? Why was it written? Why did the speaker, or writer, use certain words or images?
- **When** was the passage written? When did the action take place?
- **How** is the passage put together? How would the original listeners/readers have responded? How can I apply the message of this passage to my life?
- **Who** wrote the passage? Who appears in it? Who is the writer talking to?
- **Where** did the action take place? Where was it written? Where do all the odd socks go?

use some help

None of us, however expert we are, can expect to understand all the Bible straight away. While a lot of the Bible is pretty straightforward in its meaning, sometimes the passages are a lot more obscure. So get hold of a good Bible companion or Bible guide.* If you want to look at a particular book of the Bible in more depth, you might want to get hold of a commentary. If you *really* want to take it further, you might want to learn Hebrew and Greek, take a Doctorate in Biblical Studies, spend fifteen years studying 'Dried Fruit in the Works of the Exilic Prophets' and finally go on to teach Dialectic Theology at the University of BadenBadenBaden-Wurttemflügenhavengartstadt. Unlikely, but you never know.

do some scribbling (1)

Write notes. Scribble your thoughts on this book. Underline things in your Bible (or, if you don't want to do that, put in stickers or Post-it notes). Put down your questions so you can go back to them later. Write a letter. Write a poem. Write a play. We're exploring the Bible here, and any good explorer takes notes as they go along.

do some scribbling (2)

Want to go beyond words? Express your thoughts about the topic under discussion in visual ways. Draw a picture. Make a painting. Find photos or images from papers and magazines and make a collage. Construct a 75-foot-high angel out of old scaffolding poles, discarded tyres and some Plasticene. Become professor of Large Angel Construction at the University of BadenBadenBaden-Wurttemflügenhavengartstadt.

keep a prayer journal/diary/palmtopfile

Write down what you pray for. That way you'll be able to see when – and how – God answers your prayers. You'll also be able to nudge him again on those still pending.

write your own psalm

Many psalms follow a similar basic format. You can write your own psalm by filling in the blanks in the following template. Just be honest – the psalm-writers were.

*Such as *The Bible Book* by Nick Page, HarperCollins, £11.99. Sorry. Just couldn't resist it.

Fill in the blanks

Lord, today I feel . . . (e.g. happy, sad, confused, etc.)

I know that you are . . . (e.g. caring, unchanging, very big, etc.)

And I remember that you have . . . (e.g. saved me, answered my prayers, etc.)

So I will . . . (e.g. praise you, trust in you, walk with you, etc.)

pray

We've added 'connect' prayers at the end of each topic in this book: one-word prayers that you can use to trigger your own. You might just want to leave it at one word (fine, especially if delivered with passion). You might start with that word and continue using your own words. But whatever you do, pray. Pray for yourself. Pray for others. Pray for the world. And, most of all, pray for the Theology Faculty at the University of BadenBadenBaden-Wurttemflügenhavengartstadt; they need all the help they can get.

share with others (1)

Share your explorations with those around you. Share your journey with those in your church, housegroup or youth group. Meet with friends and look at these passages and topics together. Two heads are better than one.*

share with others (2)

Introducing the 'Word Out' campaign.

If you've got a copy of *the street bible,* maybe it's time to give it away. Here's the simple plan:

1. Talk about God (at their request) to a non-Christian friend, relative or complete stranger at a bus-stop.
2. Give them your copy of *the street bible.*
3. Then write to Rob at roblacey@thestreetbible.com saying, 'I gave mine away to a pagan after a (minimum) 3-minute conversation about God and stuff. Please send me a replacement *street bible* for a third off (+ p. & p.) as part of the Word Out programme.'
4. Sit back and wait for further details.
5. Rinse and repeat.

*Although not if they're attached to the same neck. Apart from anything else, it makes choosing a tie very difficult.

In an hour

(These stats all happen in the UK every hour)

In an hour we make a fifth of a double-decker bus
And the tax man takes four million from us.
In an hour one million goes to charity
And double that to VAT.
In an hour half a Porsche gets on the road
But more than half the price is probably owed.
In an hour we're all another hour old
And the OAPs are feeling cold.
In an hour – a hundred tonnes of chocolate sold
And the zit attack is taking its hold.
But in an hour we can afford to grin
We've grown a hundred square metres of brand new skin.
In an hour there are three accused of rape.
We spend a hundred grand trying to change our shape,
We spend the same amount on changing our hair
And over a million on what we wear.
In an hour six Girl Guides retire.
One person is the victim of a serious fire.
In an hour we smoke twelve million fags,
Spend 700 grand on books and mags,
Make half a million pounds' worth of British cars
And spend the same amount on beer in bars,
Save 600 grand for a rainy day,
And much the same amount is gambled away.
Five million people talking on the phone
But no official figures for those without a home.

A hundred people join the dole.
We buy 200 grand's worth of toilet roll.
Seventeen marriages join them down the pan,
Man blames woman, woman blames man,
That's thirty-four people now divorcee,
A third on the grounds of adultery.
Five hundred *Mayfairs* leave the shelf,
Thirty-one abortions on the National Health,
Two more people amputees
And a hundred unwanted pregnancies.
In an hour seventy-three meet their final hour.
Seventy-three meet their final hour
Seventy-three meet their final hour
And here we are
With God's great power
Living in
An ivory tower.

So let's abseil down the walls of the ivory tower (caution: slippery), and take some right lifestyle down on to the streets . . .

Charity shop

street life

I remember catching the bus to go meet my girlfriend, looking the biz: smart shoes from Oxfam next to Woolies, chinos from British Heart Foundation near the post office, a Next shirt from Sue Ryder, ironically, 'Next' door. Realize the whole kit cost me £12.97. Which was less than my silk boxers!

street bible

Philippians 4:12-13

> I can relate to being totally skint. I can understand being loaded. But wherever I am in the cash spectrum, I'm happy – I've learned the knack. If I'm starving or stuffed full, bedsit-scumming it or penthouse posing – whatever, I'm happy. Now I've got God's energy – direct inject – there's no limits to what I can do.

street wise

Charity shops are great. But let's face it, charity shops would never exist if we didn't have too much stuff in the first place. Think about it. If you have a shop selling donated goods, you have to have enough stuff to give away.

Books, clothes, old LPs, bits and pieces; the detritus of everyday life, all the flotsam that is washed up on the beach of Western society. Isn't it amazing just how much unnecessary stuff there is in the world?

So maybe we should think before we buy. Buy from charity shops if that's what you want; after all, the profit goes to help those who *need* money, not those who merely want it. But don't get suckered into buying stuff you don't need, just because it's cheap. Don't fool yourself that you're only doing it 'to help the needy'. You can help them without accumulating loads of stuff. We can often harm ourselves, while all the time convinced we're doing ourselves a favour.

Matthew 6:24–34; Luke 12:13–21; Acts 2:41–47; Hebrews 10:33–35; James 2:1–9

Have nothing in your house that you do not consider to be beautiful or know to be useful. *–William Morris*

To try to satisfy your desires by possession is like using straw to put out a fire. *–Chinese proverb*

Lives based on 'having' are less free than lives based either on 'doing' or on 'being'. *–William James*

Theirs is an endless road, a hopeless maze, who seek for goods before they seek for God. *–St Bernard of Clairvaux*

what if?

Look around your life; is there stuff you can get rid of?

How would charities raise funds if we didn't have cupboards stuffed with clothes to give away?

Does this mean it's good to buy way too much stuff in the name of charity?

What motivates you to choose certain clothing? Do you buy clothes because of the looks or because of the labels?

straight ahead

Next time you buy something in a charity shop, pay double and watch the old lady faint.

When you buy something new, throw out something old. Bought a new pair of trousers? Give an old pair away.*

Go into a charity shop and buy something. When you get outside the shop, take the price tag off, then take your purchase back in and donate it to the shop. Watch the old lady faint again.

Go through your wardrobe. If there's stuff you haven't worn for a year, maybe that's a sign you don't really need it any more.

Don't say 'I need it' when you really just want it.

way out!

Repeat out loud, 'I am what I own' until you forget all the above.

Carry on shopping as before. Go out and grab those labels.

Never go to the developing world, not even for a holiday.

'O Lord, *what?*... Amen!'

*Make sure you're not wearing them at the time.

Latte

street life

I'm sitting here reading the fair-trade leaflet assuring me that my latte is guilt-free. Five years ago you could only get coffee bought at rip-off prices from desperate cash-crop farmers in the Third World. Now, we've flexed our consumer biceps and muscled our way towards Coffee-with-a-Conscience. And will we stop at that? No, my friends! We will not stop until the milk in my latte is from happy cows: cows whose milk has never touched a nonbiodegradable plastic bottle; cows who've never been force-fed GM grass; cows who . . . (I realize I'm standing on the table and everybody's staring at me). Sorry. Carry on. I've just got a thing about cows.

street bible

Amos 5:11, 21-24

'You step on the poor. You tie them in so they've got to sell to you at rock-bottom prices.

God says, 'Can't stand your religion – it turns my stomach. I detest your meetings. Yeah, fine, you bring me your offerings by the book, but I'll throw them back in your smug faces. You bring me your peace offerings, but they mean nothing; so I'll ignore them. Oh, and your songs: just shut up: they're doing my head in! If I hear one more tambourine I'm going to scream. What I want to hear is the roaring river of justice sweeping through your towns. What I want is for the right things you do to wash away the dry, hard, crusted build-up of evil.'

street wise

What we do makes a difference. What we drink matters. Coffee is not just froth, it's a pointer to where our values are.

So, look at the coffee. Who made it? Who produced it? Who grew the beans? How much are they getting out of it?

And it's not just coffee. Which sweatshop produced those jeans you're wearing? Which twelve-year-old kid worked a fourteen-hour day to make your trainers? See what you can find out: where the things came from, what the company's policy is.

Don't just buy coffee, buy justice. And if you can't buy fairly, maybe you should just say bye-bye.

Exodus 23:6; Deuteronomy 16:19; 1 Kings 3:11; Psalm 9:8, 11:7, 72:2; Ecclesiastes 5:19; Isaiah 1:15–17, 61:1–3; Luke 10:7; 1 Timothy 5:18; Revelation 19:11

Grande triple-shot latte with a vanilla syrup, please. *–Rob Lacey*

I'll have the same as him. With a straw. *–Nick Page*

The rich would have to eat money
if the poor did not provide food. *–Russian proverb*

Never before have so many people had so much in common, but never before have the things that divide them been so obvious. *–Shridath Ramphal*

sign posts

What if all coffee producers were paid a fair price for their coffee?

What difference would it make to your life if you only bought fairly traded goods?

Does your church/youth group/housegroup/crypto-anarchist cell use fairly traded products whenever possible?

what if?

Look for the fair-trade sign on goods and then buy them.

Get informed. Try to find out where the goods you buy come from.

Spend eight hours locked in the cupboard under the stairs working at a sewing machine. Now you know what a sweatshop feels like.*

Write to your local supermarket and encourage them to stock more fair-trade goods.

Shop locally where possible – support your local businesses.

If your church/youth group/housegroup/crypto-anarchist cell does not use fairly traded products, chain yourself to your vicar/youth leader/housegroup leader/Revolutionary Class Warrior until they promise to do so.

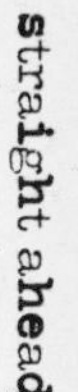

Say to yourself, 'It's dog eat dog out there.'

Get so caffeined up that you can claim diminished responsibility.

Go halfway, buy all your coffee from a Fayre . . . off a tray.

way out!

'O Lord, *please* . . . Amen!'

*Especially if that's where the central heating boiler is.

BINMEN

street life

I did a shocking thing. I said 'Thanks' to a binman. It wasn't even outside my own house. Was he shocked!

Do the angels who dispose of our spiritual mess also feel undervalued? Do these working-class angels get their wings in a flap at our lack of gratitude? Do they moan about not being appreciated when they're delivering all our gunk to the landfill site at the other end of space? Do they work their heavenly butts off clearing away stuff they know would fester and cause disease if left on our doorsteps? Do they deliberately make a row so we know they're doing their job (allegedly)? Or is there so much mess they just quietly get on with the job?

street bible

Romans 6:11-14

Likewise, count yourself as dead to the mess, and live your life facing towards God – full on, standing toe to toe. And don't let the mess call the shots, so that you're just a puppet, pulled into all sorts of stuff that's part of the old you – forced to dance to whatever's on the ghetto blaster. Cut the strings. Pull the power. Wake up. Get a life; then offer that new lease of life to God, so he can use it to make good things happen. The mess is not your boss, 'cos you're not answering to the Rules but to God's gifts, delivered with freedom included.

street wise

OK. Quick quiz question. Who is more valuable to society: a chat-show host or a binman?

Strange, isn't it, how the people who we really need get relatively little attention while those who can't be called necessary get all the plaudits.

In our lives as well, the important stuff often gets overlooked. Are the top Christians the ones up the front, leading the worship or preaching the word or wandering around in a big hat and a fancy robe? Not sure about that. Maybe God values the rest of us just as much – those who can show friendship, the peacemakers, the good neighbours.

So don't overlook the less showy stuff. Friendship, caring, praying, talking, forgiving – all these are tasks that are vital to our Christian lives. Not glamorous, maybe. Not high profile. But without them we wouldn't be able to live our Christian lives for all the garbage cluttering our path.

Psalm 51, 103:11–12; Isaiah 6:5–7; Zechariah 3:1–7; John 1:29; Romans 6:15–18

The true measure of a man is how he treats someone who can do him absolutely no good. –*Ann Landers*

There are no menial jobs, only menial attitudes. –*William Bennett*

We cannot do great things. We can only do little things with great love. –*Mother Teresa*

sign posts

what if?

What if there were no binmen? What would you do with all the rubbish?

What kinds of people are undervalued in society?

Are there vital things in your life that you don't pay enough attention to?

What if everyone had to do job experience, not just school pupils? Like, lawyers spending a week on the bins. Doctors having to sweep the gutters.

Write down the people, things, activities that mean the most to you. Pray about them.

Tell someone important in your life *why* you think they're so important.

If there are things you have identified in your Christian life that you are not paying enough attention to, schedule time for them. Make time for friendship in your diary. Make an appointment to pray.

Don't be fooled by the world's values. Treat everyone equally. Respect everyone.

straight ahead

way out!

Don't put the wheelie bins out on the pavement.

Whenever anyone questions you, ask, 'Do you know who I am?' in a loud, self-important voice.

'O Lord, *them* . . . Amen!'

LABELS

street life

I just sent off a whole load of invoices to a wide range of high street brand names for the advertising I've done recently for their clothes. Over the last five years I've kept stats on the hours I've spent wearing these different companies' products and the number of people I've been seen by during these times, and I've also got photographic documentation on just how cool and influential I looked on each of these occasions. Being so dead trendy, it all tots up to quite a bill which, when they pay up, I intend to spend on setting up my own fashion design outlet. Shouldn't be long now as I enclosed a stamped addressed envelope.

street bible

Colossians 3:12b-14

Clothes are a big statement, so let's see you sporting an image that reflects the New You: compassion suits you, kindness goes with the colours of your soul, humility sets you off nicely, gentleness is so 'you', patience is perfect with your complexion. It all fits so well, Tailor made. Bite your lip when someone crosses a line. Wipe it off the record as *your* slate's been wiped by the Boss. But you're still undressed without the finishing touch – love. Love holds all the stitches together, love makes it all look just right, love transforms an outfit into a statement.

street wise

Labels. Don't you just love them? The great thing about labels is you don't have to have any taste of your own. All you have to do is wear the right label and there you go. Instant fashion.

Of course, the really annoying thing about labels is when they're just that. You know, you pick up an Armani jacket and there's just this little, discreet label inside. You don't want that. You want a whacking great label plastered across the back that says, 'ARMANI. *I'VE* GOT IT AND *YOU* HAVEN'T.'

Have you ever wondered, though, if Jesus wore labels. Did he get his robes at Ralph Lauren? Did he buy his sandals at Timberland? (He had a disciple called Levi, but the New Testament doesn't mention if the guy ran a jeans factory.) Did he say, 'No man builds a tower without first wearing Lacoste'?

Don't think so. Instead he told us not to worry about appearance. He told us not to pay attention to those kind of things. The only label we should want to wear reads, 'Made by God. Washed in love.'

Psalm 45:3; Proverbs 31:25; Isaiah 61:10; Matthew 6:25–34; Luke 24:49; Romans 13:14; Galatians 3:27; 1 Peter 5:5

Beware of all enterprises that require new clothes.
–Henry David Thoreau

I wear my sort of clothes to save me the trouble of deciding which clothes to wear.
–Katharine Hepburn

Be careless in your dress if you must, but keep a tidy soul.
–Mark Twain

The bread that you withhold belongs to the poor; the cape that you hide in your chest belongs to the naked; the shoes rotting in your closet belong to those who must go unshod.
–Basil of Caesarea

sign posts

what if?

Do you take any notice of labels?

Are you affected by what is fashionable?

When will we reach the point when it's all label and no actual clothing?

Imagine if Nike sponsored the original Ten Commandments – 'Just don't do it.'

Buy fairly traded clothing if possible.

Buy things you like, not things you're supposed to like.

Appreciate beauty, not ostentation.

Buy an Adidas cover for your Bible.

Wear your clothes inside out so that everyone can see the label.

'O Lord, *which?* . . . Amen!'

bUS

street life

On the bus to town. This woman sits next to me (hurrumph) and then starts chatting (argh!). Of course, it comes round to her asking me, 'D'you work?' I lied. Said I work in a bank. Should I have told her I work for a church? No, it might've started something about her not being religious but how she's always believed in God and she's always quite liked Jesus and how it's a shame he died and why did they have to kill him like that and has it got anything to do with her eternal soul. And you don't want that, do you?! Not when you're tired and you've got an evangelism planning meeting to go to.

street bible

Acts 8:26-39

[The story so far . . . Phil's on a mission, sent by Unspecified Angel Officer to hang out with the Ethiopian Palace Treasurer no less. The guy's heading home in his top-of-the-range Chariot, fired up and deep into the Good Book.]

Phil bounds up to the side of the wheel hubs and listens in: the guy's reading out loud from Isaiah. The Treasurer asks Phil, 'Who's the courier on about? Is it autobiographical, fiction, non-fiction? What?' Phil grabs the chance with both hands and works from this bit through all the rest of the Instruction Manual with brilliant apologetics about the fantastic breaking news on Jesus.

They pass an outdoor swimming pool and the Treasurer says, 'Water! What's stopping me getting baptized?' Phil does the honours and baptizes the guy right there.

street wise

'It's good to talk' ran the old British Telecom advert. But it's even better to listen. People, you see, have problems. Questions. Ideas. Comments. So one of the great things we can do is listen. Help them to sort things out. Show them a few pointers to the right bus to get on.

Shame then that so often we prefer to talk at them rather than to them. We want to do EVANGELISM: bombard them with our beliefs, rather than chat.

Jesus talked. Jesus listened. Jesus asked questions. Talking to people, really talking to people, means sharing in their lives. Dialogues rather than monologues. Real conversations with real people about what really matters.

Genesis 12:1; 2 Kings 7:3–9; Mark 14:66–72; Luke 24:13–35; Acts 9, 17:1–4; 2 Timothy 4:5; 1 Peter 3:15

sign posts

Good communication is as stimulating as black coffee*, and just as hard to sleep after. *–Anne Morrow Lindbergh*

Not only to say the right thing in the right place, but, far more difficult, to leave unsaid the wrong thing at the tempting moment. *–George Sala*

In the midst of a generation screaming for answers, Christians are stuttering. *–Howard Hendricks*

what if?

Do you ever talk about the Bible with people? Or do you think it won't interest them?

When was the last time you talked to a non-Christian about your faith?

How good would it be if someone's reading the Bible (street or proper) on the bus, they turn the page and the person who's been reading it over their shoulder from the seat behind says, 'Whoa, I'm not done with that page yet'?

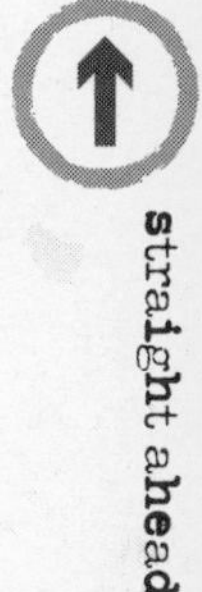

straight ahead

Deep conversation requires time. Make time to talk to your friends. Go to the pub/café/drinks machine, get them round for a meal, turn off your mobile and listen.

When people talk to you, be interested in their lives. God is.

Take the initiative, break the ice, see if they're actually happy to chat.

When trying to steer the conversation towards God stuff, don't grab the steering wheel, just point out the signposts towards Godville. See if they're into a quick tour.

way out!

Wear headphones . . . and sing along.

Avoid eye contact: stare straight forward. Better still, wear shades.

Tell them you're a Hare Krishna: Plain Clothes Division.

Never answer people's questions. Instead, always give them the answer you prepared earlier.

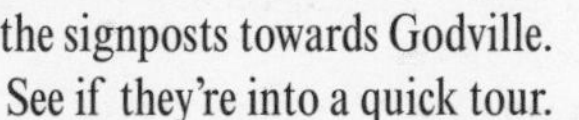

'O Lord, *when?* . . . Amen!'

*Which makes talking with a bore a 'decaf conversation'.

GRAffITI

street life

It was just a name on a wall. But it was one of the best, most artistic, expressive pieces of art I've ever seen on the streets, in a gallery, in a museum, anywhere. An in-yer-face gesture of confidence, self-assurance and sheer guts. An exotic explosion of colour and shape. An explosion of beauty on the brickwork. Beautiful.

Just a shame his name was 'Bernard'.

street bible

Exodus 36:2-5

Moses calls them all up on stage; all those God had endowed with skills. Everyone who's up for it charges forward. Moses donates all the bulging collection bags and it's all allocated to the job of making God's Retreat Place special. But the Jews just kept on writing out the cheques, every morning the office in-tray is full of top-up donations. The artists down tools and go to Moses. 'Tell them to stop funding us so generously, we've got too much sponsorship money for making God's plans for the project happen.'

So Moses sends round an official memo, 'Whoa! No one's to make any more contributions for the Retreat Centre.' So the reins were pulled back on people's financial commitment to the project, 'cos they already had surpassed the spending budget.

street wise

OK, let's get the standard response out of the way. Grafitti is anti-social behaviour. It's vandalism.

Fair enough, if you're talking about private houses, or shops or beautiful facades. Fair enough if the kind of graffiti we're discussing is ugly slogans, mindless damage or the symbols of hate.

But then there's that other kind. Sudden explosions of colour in the concrete desert. Technicolor creativity, large-scale art, personal expressions that work the other way, brightening up a dull terrain, bringing to life soulless concrete and stone.

Maybe in our drab and colourless lives we need to be a bit more creative, a bit more wild, a bit less responsible. Occasionally we need to take the dull wall of our faith and just get the spray can out.

Exodus 31:1–11; Numbers 24:5; Joshua 7:21; Psalm 48:2; Proverbs 24:4; Ecclesiastes 3:11; Song of Songs 1:10, 11; Isaiah 28:1–5; Jeremiah 6:2; Lamentations 2:15; Ezekiel 16:12, 27:4; Daniel 11:16; Luke 21:5; Acts 3:2; Romans 1:20

sign posts

Art is the signature of man. *–G. K. Chesterton*

Where the spirit does not work with the hand, there is no art. *–Leonardo da Vinci*

All great art is the expression of man's delight in God's work, not his own. *–John Ruskin*

what if?

What if art isn't just for certain types, but also for the not-so-certain types?

What do you do that is creative? How can you use that to worship God?

Does your church employ and support artists? If not, why not?

Why is it that in most churches, Christian art doesn't go beyond banner-making?

straight ahead

Save up, buy some real art.

Support your local Christian artist.

Take up poetry or painting or pottery or any other art. (Even if it doesn't begin with the letter 'p'.)
Use it to say something about God . . . or whatever.

See if it's possible to create some Christian art that doesn't feature (a) a cross (b) a fish or (c) some cute kittens in a basket.

Build a wall for people to paint.

way out!

Whenever you meet an artist tell them that they are an idolater.

Just have crappy plastic flowers.

Grow accustomed to the Joy of Grey.

Always ensure any poster of the glory of God's creation has a Bible text in the bottom right-hand corner justifying it.

Don't even doodle in the margin without adding a Bible reference.

'O Lord, *aha!* . . . Amen!'

KISS

street life

Trendy Couple are sitting outside the coffee house getting stuck into a cappuccino-flavoured kiss. Sad thing is, I hear myself think, 'Not been going out long, then.' Then my brain starts playing tricks on me. It reruns the same scene with a couple in their seventies having a good ol' snog. Then it's my parents! Argh!! But then I guess they must've done all that stuff, and more . . . at least once. Quick, think of something else!

street bible

1 Corinthians 13:4-8

> What is love anyway? Not the tripe you've been force-fed! No, love gives people space and time; it does people good. It's not jealous, loud-mouthed or cocky. It's not vulgar; it doesn't look after No. 1. It's not got a short fuse – it forgives and forgets. Love doesn't smile when dark stuff goes on, but throws a party when the truth gets out. It protects more than a blockbuster hero; it trusts more than a toddler. It's always positive; it always hangs in there. Love doesn't let you down.

street wise

God is a romantic. (Has to be: he invented men and women.) You don't invent roses if you're not a hopeless romantic. You don't invent warm summer evenings if you're not expecting people to fall in love. You don't invent hands without considering the possibility that human beings might hold them. You don't invent lips without understanding that quite a lot of people would do more with them than just talk.

But God is also a realist. (Has to be: he invented reality.) So in his view, romance has to be grounded in responsibility. In his world romance is part of relationships: it's not a shortcut to personal gratification, it's a gift to someone you love.

So don't use romance as a way to play with people's emotions, don't kiss and run; treat people as you would want to be treated.

And look for the romantic in everyday life. Hollywood romances are all very well, but they never tell you the whole story. A little bit of romance in life, a show of affection, can sparkle through the whole week. A bunch of flowers, breakfast in bed; schmaltzy, we know, but not if they're done with meaning, not if they're tokens of a greater, stronger, deeper love.

Proverbs 24:26, 27:6; Matthew 22:37–40; Luke 22:48; Romans 16:16; oh, and dare we suggest the whole of Song of Songs?

sign posts

Love does not consist of gazing at each other, but in looking outward together in the same direction. *–Antoine de Saint-Exupéry*

We've got this gift of love, but love is like a precious plant. You can't just accept it and leave it in the cupboard or just think it's going to get on by itself. You've got to keep watering it; really look after it and nurture it. *–John Lennon*

I met in the street a very poor young man who was in love. His hat was old, his coat threadbare, the water passed through his shoes, and the stars through his soul. *–Victor Hugo*

what if?

Do we need to be in a relationship to be happy?

Are there people you have hurt? Have you been hurt yourself? How could the situation have been handled better?

'All you need is love.' Discuss.

What's the difference between a 'holy kiss' and a 'proper kiss'?*

Take your wife/husband/significant other out on a date. (Never mind how long you've been together.)

Treat people with dignity and care: don't just 'use 'em and lose 'em'.

way out!

Never commit yourself.

Don't say, 'I love you.' Say, 'I think you might be a suitable biological mating partner.'

If you must give your partner flowers, the local cemetery always has some going spare.

Once the Chase and the Kiss have happened, keep looking round for other options.

Download a prenuptial agreement from the web and check the get-out clauses.

'O Lord, *advise* . . . Amen!'

*About two minutes.

BIllbOArd

street life

'He wouldn't endorse it if he didn't use it himself in real life.'
'That's such a funny advert that I'm going out right now to buy one.'
'If I clean my teeth with that, I'll be able to throw away my brace and have perfect teeth like her.'
'If I use that shampoo, my torso will miraculously alter shape in the shower.'
'I've seen that advert so often, I *am* David Beckham.'

street bible

Romans 12:1-2

So I say – and I can't say it strong enough – with all this 'God writing off our mess' in mind: give it up for God – your life; give it up. Like sacrifices, only live ones. Put your body on the butcher's block, your neck in the noose and let God's hands hold the controls. This is what 'being spiritual' means; this is 'worship'– making God smile. Don't get moulded by what the adverts say you should have / should do / should be. Keep on becoming more and more outstanding – literally, standing out, as your thinking's freshened up, regular. Then you'll know what God wants for you. What his plan is for your life – the plan that can't be criticized.

street wise

The strange thing about car adverts is that there's never anyone else on the road. The streets are deserted or the car is speeding along some remote stretch of country road or crossing a distant desert. There's never anyone around. (Apart from the occasional elk, which the car swerves effortlessly to avoid.) It's the algebra of persuasion: 'me + cars = freedom'. Buy this car and there will always be a clear road ahead.

See, life is sweet in Ad-land. Everyone's happy because they're wearing the right jeans or drinking the right beer. And if they're not happy, it's because they bought the wrong brand of goods and are therefore despised and rejected and tragically unhip.

Get real. Buying a car won't buy you freedom. Wearing the 'right' clothes won't make you more attractive; smoking those cigarettes won't turn you into a cowboy and using that credit card will not solve all of your problems.

Buy what you want, but always, always ask questions of the adverts. Because in Ad-land nothing is real. Not even the elk.*

*If you freeze the frame and zoom in, you can quite clearly see the costume has a zip. And the antlers are stuck on with Blu-tack.

streetlights

Genesis 6:2; 1 Samuel 16:6–7; Esther 1:11; Mark 3:33, 34; 1 Corinthians 2:1–5; 2 Corinthians 5:20

signposts

It used to be that people needed products to survive. Now products need people to survive.

–Nicholas Johnson

You can tell the ideals of a nation by its advertisements.

–Norman Douglas

Advertisers in general bear a large part of the responsibility for the deep feelings of inadequacy that drive women to psychiatrists, pills or the bottle.

–Marya Manne

Living in an age of advertisement, we are perpetually disillusioned.

–J.B. Priestley

what if?

Is all advertising wrong?

What's the difference between a good advert and a bad advert?

Have you ever bought something just because you liked the advert?

How did you hear about this book?

- ☐ I saw it on the shelf.
- ☐ I was given it to celebrate my birthday/bar mitzvah/ appendectomy.
- ☐ I saw an advert in a magazine.
- ☐ A hand appeared and wrote *'Mene, mene,* go and buy *street life'* on my bedroom wall.

Are you a good advert for God?

straight ahead!

Think.

way out!

Don't think.

'O Lord, *guilty* . . . Amen!'

Penthouse

street life

It used to be a tatty old seventies office block. Now it's got itself a face lift: an injection of industrial botox between the brickwork. A plastic surgeon of the construction industry has waved his spirit level over it and today it's 'a luxury apartment complex with views across the city to the bay'. I've blagged my way to a view of the Penthouse Apartment Showroom, and I've realized I really could get my spiritual life together here. I'd be able to pray so much more effectively for the city with a view like this. It'd prove to non-Christians that successful people also need God. I could witness to all the other leaseholders. And open-plan rooms are so much more suited to the housegroup strategy. I need this apartment!

street bible

Habakkuk 3:16b-19

Whatever happens, I'll celebrate God, party in my heart 'cos he liberates me. Even if the shelves are bare, even if the cupboards are empty, I'll party, celebrate God. When the projects fail, when the screen goes blank, I'll party, celebrate God. He liberates me. The God who runs the cosmos is what keeps me going. He makes my every step as sure-footed as a deer on the mountains. I can climb because of his energy and protection.

street wise

Life at street level can get you down. What we really need is something out of TV makeover land. A Lottery-sized win to lift us away from the here and now; a converted barn in southern France, a Tuscan olive grove, a new 4x4 lifestyle with electric windows, air-con and chrome-plated luxury.

Nothing wrong with dreams, of course, nothing wrong with having aims and ambitions, places we want to go, things we want to do. But are they the right dreams? Are they dreams that will make our life more meaningful? Or are we just dreaming of escape?

Sometimes, our dreams cripple us in the here and now. Maybe we should wake up and smell the tarmac. There is life to be lived wherever we are. Jesus was born in a cowshed, not a castle. Dreams are good places to visit, but you wouldn't want to live there.

streetlights

Job 36:11; Proverbs 13:25, 19:23; Ecclesiastes 4:8; Philippians 4:12–13; 1 Timothy 6:6, 8; Hebrews 13:5

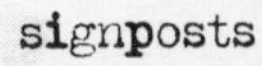

signposts

Every eel hopes to become a whale.

–German proverb

We act as though comfort and luxury were the chief requirements of life, when all that we need to make us really happy is something to be enthusiastic about.

–Charles Kingsley

Luxuries are what other people buy.

–David White

what if?

What are your dreams? What do you want to do with your life?

What things make you envious of other people? Why do you feel this way?

Can an over-active jealousy gland be treated on the NHS?

Are some people called to poverty? Or is that a cop-out?

straight ahead!

Make a list of all you possess. Everything. See if you finish the task.

Make a list of what you want out of life. Now ask God what he thinks of the list.

way out!

Get a credit card and go for it.

Remind yourself that 'Greed is Good'.

Always go for the highest-paid job you can – even if you like what you're doing.

Never be satisfied.

'O Lord, *hurrumph!* . . . Amen!'

Credit Card

street life

I almost wish I'd kept them. All those letters that come through the post offering me new credit cards, free transfers and 0 per cent interest for the first six months. I should write back, thanking them kindly for the chance to pay exorbitant amounts of my limited resources so I can go even further into debt, with the added bonus of paying my bank manager every time he decides to get in touch about my bouncy cheques and getting to know pain specialists Bruiser Bailiffs. As for the free gift with another credit card: I'll take the handy overnight bag, as this'll be more useful to me when I'm sleeping on the streets.

street bible

1 Timothy 6:6-8, 10

Being like God *will* make you rich – but not (necessarily) in money terms. Isn't 'rich' not needing anything else? Isn't 'rich' being happy with what you've got? Are we born with a bulging wallet of readies? Nope. Has anyone found the exchange rate for swapping cash into heaven-dollars? Nope. But if we've got clothes to cover our skin and food to fill it with – great!

Download the mental image of a huge 'Tree of Evil', branches dripping with rancid fruit. Dig up the roots, hack them apart and what d'you find? This love affair with money is the sap oozing through the whole thing, feeding it, nourishing it. The fruit's poisoned many people's conviction; they've drifted off, doubled up with gut rot.

street wise

It's so easy, isn't it? Just slide that strip of plastic across the counter and take the goods home. It's painless, simple, consequence-free spending. Well, no, actually. It's a snare, a velvet cage, a trap so smoothly designed that you can hardly feel the jaws as they close around you.

Debt is a burden that cripples so many people. And it only works because we want things too easily, and we don't want to wait. And the banks, the building society, the credit agencies, they don't want you to wait either. They want you to jump in without thinking, because that way you'll end up paying them lots more money.

So think before you spend. Count the cost before you shell out. Can you afford it? Do you really need it? And how much is it really going to cost?

streetlights

Deuteronomy 15:1–3; 2 Kings 4:7; Nehemiah 10:31; Job 24:1–12; Habakkuk 2:7; Matthew 6:12, 18:21–35; Luke 7:36–50

signposts

Credit buying is much like being drunk.
The buzz happens immediately, and it gives you a lift.
The hangover comes the day after.

–Joyce Brothers

Debt is the worst poverty.

–Thomas Fuller

Some people use one half their ingenuity to get into debt, and the other half to avoid paying it.

–George D. Prentice

what if?

What's so bad about a credit card?

Have a look in your purse/wallet/secret compartment. How many credit cards or store cards do you have?

Why is it that we can't wait for things?

Does God offer us a credit card with a difference? You get all the good things he's got for you and Jesus pays off your monthly statement. If so, what's your credit limit?*

straight ahead!

Stop spending on your credit cards.

If you can't stop using them, then cut up your credit cards.

Every time you get some junk mail offering you a new card, don't throw away the return envelope. Instead, stuff it with some of your other junk mail and send it back to them.

way out!

Get another credit card today. And go platinum if you can!

'O Lord, *scary* . . . Amen!'

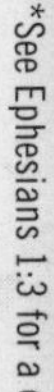

*See Ephesians 1:3 for a clue.

gym

street life

I've got too much work, I've got no time, I'm too tired, I'm allergic to my own sweat, I'll go tomorrow, I can't find my shorts, I look daft in Lycra, it's raining and I'll catch a cold, I've got a cold already, I'm in between colds, I can't miss *A Question of Sport*, it's ages since I've gone, I might pull a muscle, I don't want to look too muscular anyway, the lads are down the pub, it's rude not to be sociable, they're all getting fat, they'd feel bad if I got a six-pack, four-pack, two-pack, could pack my bag without breaking sweat. So not today then.

street bible

2 Timothy 2:1-7

So, my boy, use your spiritual muscle on the gifts God's given you since you connected with the Liberator Jesus. What you've picked up from me, hand on down to solid guys who can coach others. Tough it out with us, like crack army units in the Liberator Jesus' taskforce. Trained combat teams don't get sucked into the daily soap opera of normal life. No, the only thing that counts is the nod of approval from their officer in charge. Or if you're more into sport: the athlete doesn't get the gold if he's taken a short cut. Or agriculture: the farmer who sticks in the hours and pays out in sweat – he's the one who gets to spend the profits. Think about it! The Boss'll turn the lights on for you.

street wise

I've often thought about running the London marathon. Well, not exactly running it – finishing it. You know, burst through the tape, arms held aloft in glory. Yeah, I like that bit. It's the running bit I can't be doing with. Maybe I could do it on a bike. Or in a taxi.

See, we like the finishing bits. We like the glory parts of life, the good things. But we don't like the struggle to get there. But, you can't get fit if you don't exercise. You can't reach the mountain-tops if you don't conquer the valleys.

So don't let anyone tell you that being a Christian is always easy. It's not like that. Faith is often a struggle. At those points we've got two choices: either give up the race or keep running. There isn't any other choice.

You can't coast along as a Christian. There is no spiritual taxi to whisk us easily to our destination. No. Just two choices: give up or run the race.

Your choice.

Proverbs 3:11–12; Hebrews 12:1–13; 1 Timothy 4:8; 2 Timothy 4:6–8

sign posts

Most people run a race to see who is fastest.
I run a race to see who has the most guts.
–Steve Prefontaine

No pain, no gain.* *–Anon*

By perseverance the snail reached the ark. *–Charles Spurgeon*

Whenever I feel like exercise
I lie down until the feeling passes.
–Robert M. Hutchins

Some of the world's greatest feats were accomplished by people not smart enough to know they were impossible.
–Doug Larson

what if?

Do you have stickability?

Which parts of your Christian life do you find exhausting?

How can we help each other to run the race?

Why is it that 90 per cent of gym members give up going regularly within six weeks of joining?

What's the spiritual equivalent to endorphins?†

straight ahead

Do some spiritual jogging. Read your Bible. Pray. Exercise with God.

Get together with others – most people run better when they have people jogging alongside.

Book in time to do some training – write it in under 'meeting with Jim'.

way out!

Put your feet up, have a cup of tea, take it easy.

Use your trainers as a fashion accessory.

Get some exercise: run all the way to the phone and call a taxi.

'O Lord, *but* . . . Amen!'

*To which the response is: 'No pain, no pain.' †'Endorphins' – Nick didn't know either . . . look it up!

Beggar

street life

Who was he, how long's he been in this state, what went wrong? Tidy him up a bit, with a little imagination he'd look quite respectable. But he may have scars, or be chronically ill, or not quite all there. I'm intrigued. Fascinated.

'You lost, geezer? Or just plain nosey?' he says, direct at me.

The latter, I realize. 'Sorry,' I say. Then we chat. After which I think it may have been the former.

street bible

Luke 16:19-31

Another story. Two guys: a beggar and a millionaire. Both die. The beggar goes direct into Abraham's arms. The rich guy's in a torture chamber in hell. He looks up, yells, 'Abraham, give us a break. Send what's-his-name down with some water for me, I'm in agony in these flames!'

Abraham comes back, 'Sorry, but no can do! It's all-change. You had all the breaks in your previous life, and Lazarus here got the rough end of the deal. Now it's vice versa. Anyway, if he *wanted* to come down, he couldn't.'

'OK,' says the rich guy, 'send, uh . . . what was it? "Lazarus"; send him back to my five brothers. They've got to know hell's worse than the worst horror story they've heard.' Abraham shouts back down, 'So Moses and the whole list of couriers weren't good enough, huh?'

The rich guy's struggling now: 'But surely, if someone comes back from the dead, they'll be all ears.' Abraham doubts it: 'They were all mouth with Moses, and they added in hand gestures to the couriers – they're not shifting even if someone comes back from the dead!'*

street wise

Begging. It's been with humanity right from the beginning. The poor have always been around; they always will be around. You see, greed never goes away, either. And so the poor become a kind of permanent background to our societies; impossible to eradicate, easy to ignore.

Except for one single, vital fact: all those beggars, all those people living in poverty – God is their father as well. So, like it or not, we're related.

Of course, it's complicated. Fighting poverty means challenging the structures that lead to poverty – and that's a big battle. But the fact that we can't do everything is never an excuse for doing nothing. After all, we're family.

*For full version see *the street bible*.

1 Samuel 2:6–8; Isaiah 58:6–12; Amos 5:11–24; Habakkuk 2:6–20; Mark 10:46–52

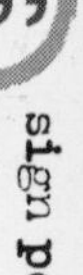

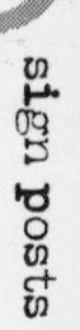

This is charity, to do all, all that we can.
–John Donne

If a free society cannot help the many who are poor, it cannot save the few who are rich.
–John F. Kennedy

It is no disgrace to be poor – which is the only good thing you can say about it.
–Jewish proverb

The poverty of our century is unlike that of any other. It is not, as poverty was before, the result of natural scarcity, but of a set of priorities imposed upon the rest of the world by the rich. Consequently, the modern poor are not pitied but written off as trash. The twentieth-century consumer economy has produced the first culture for which a beggar is a reminder of nothing.
–John Berger

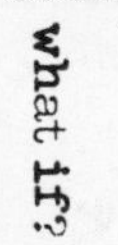

Why are people homeless?

What is the best way to help them?

How do you react when someone asks you for change?

Wherever you go in the world there will be beggars. Why do you think that is?

Ask a homeless person about their plans.

Get into conversation.

Buy the *Big Issue* (it's a good read, but buy it anyway).

Give regularly to an organization that works with the homeless.

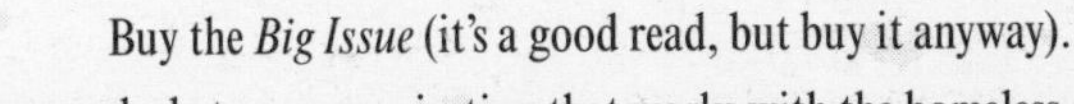

Keep your wallet in your pocket and don't look them in the eye.

The next time you see a homeless person, pop into the estate agent's and get them one of those property newspapers.

'O Lord, *change* . . . Amen!'

ROAD WORKS

street life

We are so indebted to Mr Bollard. Without the invention that he (presumably) gave his name to, where would we be? In a hole, literally. And yet, do we thank him? No. Whenever we see bollards, we mutter under our breath, tap the steering wheel and look at our watches. Why isn't our reaction more like, 'Great, they're improving the services to this street!' or 'There's been a terrible accident and things are getting sorted – I'll pray.' Nope, just a default formula: Bollards + Traffic = Delay. We don't care about dealing with difficulties or improving things. We just care about the inconvenience. When you're in a rush, there's no time to make things better. Bollards!

street bible

Matthew 3:1–3

About the same time, John 'Baptizer' Zechariahson starts getting big profile in the Judean Desert. He's getting capacity crowds with his thought-for-the-decade full-on performances. He's going, 'Turn your lives round. A full 180 degrees. 'Cos Heaven On Earth's just round the corner and you're looking the wrong way.'

Check it out . . . it's the same guy the courier Isaiah predicted:
'What's that voice? Drifting in from the wasteland,
"Give us a motorway. A straight line of lanes . . .
For God's cavalcade to really move."'

street wise

Sometimes things have to go wrong to go right. Sometimes things have to break down in order to be rebuilt again. There are times when things just don't work. Bad times, even tragic times. Times when we feel God is far away, when we feel as though we have fallen into a deep, dark hole and there is no one to lift us out.

But let's be clear: it's always been this way. Illness, bereavement, relationship breakdown – and many more shattering events – have been part of the life of human beings from the start. That's not much of a comfort. But it is true. And the Bible doesn't promise us otherwise. The question for us as Christians is not 'Will you suffer?' but 'How will you react when suffering comes?'

We can look at the troubled times in our lives negatively and start to question everything we believe in, or we can ask what God is saying through this and look to the future. We can ask God to repair our lives, put us back on track and send us off in a better direction.

Psalm 27:11, 119:32; Proverbs 2:9,13, 4:26, 15:19,24; Isaiah 2:3, 26:7; Jeremiah 6:16; Acts 2:28; Luke 1:79; 2 Corinthians 6:3; Hebrews 12:13

He who suffers much will know much. *–Greek proverb*

Disappointment often focuses on the failure of our own agenda rather than on God's long-term purposes for us, which may use stress and struggle as tools for strengthening our spiritual muscles. *–Luci Shaw*

It is a glorious thing to be indifferent to suffering, but only to one's own suffering.
–Robert Lynd

There is no man in the world without some trouble or affliction, though he be a king or a pope. *–Thomas à Kempis*

sign posts

what if?

What is causing you anxiety or pain in your life at the moment? Do you think God is saying anything to you through this? How can you use your experience to learn more about him?

What parts of your life does God need to repair? What parts does he need to tear down and rebuild?

Do you believe that God has a better future for you?

Do whatever you can to get alongside those who are suffering.

Believe that God loves you – whatever you are going through at the moment.

If it ain't broke, don't fix it.

Take two aspirins and deal with it in the morning.

Buy a job lot of plasters.

'O Lord, *me?* . . . Amen!'

CLUBBING

street life

A friend of mine is the spitting image of Jesus ('cos, of course, we know what he looked like!). Well, he has long dark hair and a beard anyway. So, as a dare, he dresses up in the white all-in-one, puts on a pair of old sandals and joins the queue outside the night club. They don't know what to make of him. 'Is it a mick take?', 'Where's the secret camera?', 'What, no VIP fast-track treatment?' But they're totally fazed when they get inside and see him strut his stuff.

street bible

John 2:3-10

Jesus' mum says to him, 'Wine's gone!' . . . She primes the drinks staff to do what Jesus says – to the word. Camera zooms to six huge jars holding about 100 litres of foot-washing water – each.

Jesus' voice echoes round them, 'Get some water, fill the jars, right up.' The drinks staff do what he says – to the word. Then Jesus tells them, 'Take them to the guy in charge of tasting.' They do.

The boss man does his wine-tasting routine. Then he asks for a quick word in the bridegroom's ear: 'I've been around; I know the normal routine. The groom has the best wine served up front and brings out the cheap stuff for when they've had too much and their taste buds are a bit shot. But you've turned it all on its head, bringing out the vintage wine *last*. Unheard of!'*

street wise

Jesus was always being criticized. (Still is, in fact.) But when he walked around Israel, all those years ago, people didn't like the way he acted. For a holy man he laughed too much, drank too much, went to too many parties; he lacked the right kind of decorum. He just didn't seem to tell people off enough.

Sometimes we confuse seriousness with sanctity; we believe that to be a Christian means to be sombre, severe, sanctimonious.† The Bible mentions 'joy' a lot. It doesn't mention 'standing around looking very boring' once.

But to be a Christian is to be joyful. And joy breaks out into movement. Joy fills our whole bodies, not just our heads. It's not foolish or frivolous to dance, to cheer, to party. It's celebrating. And we have a lot to celebrate.

Jesus has turned us all into new wine. So the question is, are you humdrum, run-of-the-mill house plonk or the bubbliest vintage champagne?

*For full version, see *the street bible*. †And other words beginning with an 's'. Except silly.

2 Samuel 6:14; Psalms 31:11, 149:3; Ecclesiastes 3:4; Matthew 11:17; Luke 7:31–35

sign posts

Joy is the most infallible sign of the presence of God.
–Leon Bloy

Dance as if no one is watching; love as if you can't be hurt.
Sing tho' no one is listening; live as if it's heaven on earth.
–Anon

Always remember, joy is not incidental to spiritual quest. It is vital.
–Rebbe Nachman

Joy is the feeling of grinning on the inside.
–Melba Colgrove

what if?

Why did Jesus spend so much time at parties?

Why does everyone get embarrassed when their parents dance?

Why, when they dance, does the average Christian look like a baboon with a hernia?

Why does 'Christian dance' have to be so obvious, especially when the words are up on that huge great screen anyway?

Dance. Go on, we dare you.

Take a crash course in tap dancing. Then, when the organist starts playing 'How Great Thou Art', spring into action.

way out!

Claim that all dancing is sinful. If people question this, perform a series of manoeuvres that will leave them in no doubt that you're right.

If you see someone in church start to clap, tie their hands together with duct tape.

Tie your laces together in case the rhythm corrupts you.

Point out the little-known spelling mistake: it wasn't 'wine', it was 'whine'.

'O Lord, *gulp!* . . . Amen!'

LitteR

street life

'You dropped this by accident!' was all I said. The fact that I'd chased him up the street was maybe a bit over-keen. The fact that he was driving a metallic-finish motor and I had to run for half a mile was also admittedly a little zealous. But I feel strongly about people who throw things out of their car windows. I know it was only an apple core, but it's the principle of the thing. The whole thing wore me out. Had to go shopping, so I took the car instead. I mean, I know I only live two hundred yards from the shop, but those disposable nappies weigh a ton.

street bible

Genesis 1:24-31

Day six: Then God says, 'Let's make people – like us, but human, with flesh and blood, skin and bone. Give them the job of caretakers of the vegetation, game wardens of all the animals.' So God makes people, like him, but human. He makes male and female. He smiles at them and gives them their job description: 'Make babies! Be parents, grandparents, great-grandparents – fill the earth with your families and run the planet well. You've got all the plants to eat from, so have all the animals – plenty for all. Enjoy.' God looks at everything he's made, and says, 'Fantastic. I love it!'

street wise

Everything's disposable these days. Use it up, wear it out, chuck it away. We fill the earth with our cast-off rubbish, clutter the streets with discarded wrappers, clog up the drains with cigarette-butts.

But the resources we use we have in trust from God. The trees that make our newspapers, the earth we open for landfill; that's not ours. That belongs to the owner. So don't use too much. Use enough. And recycle; give it back.

Recycle everything. What about the other things that God gives us? What about his love? Do we recycle that and pass it on? Or do we chuck that away into the gutter? Do we unwrap his peace and pass it around, or do we screw it up into a ball and throw it into the bin? If you're going to chuck stuff around, throw peace and grace and beauty. If you're going to litter, litter the world with love and hope.

Numbers 35:33; Psalm 24:1; Isaiah 6:3; Romans 8:18–22; Revelation 11:18

sign posts

The ground is holy, being even as it came from the Creator. Keep it, guard it, care for it, for it keeps men, guards men, cares for men. Destroy it and man is destroyed. *–Alan Paton*

Man is a complex being; he makes deserts bloom – and lakes die. *–Gil Stern*

Nature is but a name for an effect whose cause is God. *–William Cowper*

What if products had less packaging? Would you still buy them?

Have you ever just chucked something down on to the pavement?

If God has given humans this planet, surely we can just use it as we like, can't we?

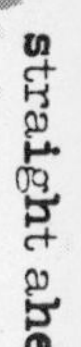

Keep all your rubbish for one week. Put it in a bag. At the end of the week weigh it. Now think how many bags of rubbish you make each month, each year, each decade. Blimey.

Recycle your rubbish. Make sure your tin, plastics and cardboard are sent to a good home.

Get into composting. Turn your vegetable rubbish back into earth. Composting is fun. Well, not exactly fun, but it's useful.*

Recycle everything. Thing every cycle re.

If you see rubbish on the ground, pick it up and put it in a bin. Even if it's not yours.

Don't just let your rubbish blow down the street in the wind. Staple it to a tree.

After reading this book, rip it into shreds and throw it out of an upstairs window.

Cling to the bit where it says, 'Earth's going to be wrapped up anyway' . . . or something like that . . . er, doesn't it?

'O Lord, *yessss!* . . . Amen!'

*I mean, some people might find it fun, but they're probably very strange people with too much facial hair and suspiciously muddy fingers.

VITAMINS

street life

The chemist's window is packed full of plastic bottles. The sign says, 'Not got time to eat properly? Pop a vitamin pill.' Next shop along is a greengrocer's. Rare these days. Seems you're only allowed in if you've got a bus pass. But I know I need my vitamins, even if I have to shortcut the process of cleaning, peeling, slicing, boiling and sometimes even chewing. No, much quicker to gulp it down with a can of fizzy caffeine. That'll keep me going. What'll keep me going with my excuse-for-a-Christian-life?

street bible

Proverbs 3:8

> Giving God respect and giving evil the cold shoulder is better than double the daily dose of vitamins and minerals.

street wise

If we're honest, most of us approach our Christian life like toddlers eating lunch. We'll gobble down the worship times, maybe taste a bit of the teaching, perhaps even have a tiny spoonful of puréed Bible study. But prayer? Don't like it. Self-discipline? Leave it on the side of the plate. Sacrificial love? Hmm. Think I'll open that bottle another day.

And so we have a vitamin-deficient Christian life, never quite as healthy as it could be, because we don't take the full daily dose. But there are no shortcuts here. No 'prayer pills' to pop to make up the deficiency. God's balanced diet involves some basic Christian foodstuffs: reading the Scriptures, praying, loving our neighbours, telling others about Jesus, learning more about the faith, fighting for justice and peace, worshipping God not just through music but through our lives.

For each of us there are likes and dislikes. But to leave some aside is to miss out on the full meal. Spiritually speaking, sometimes we just need to eat our greens. They might taste better than we think.

Proverbs 4:22, 15:30; Jeremiah 30:17, 33:6; Daniel 1:15; Zechariah 11:16; 2 Corinthians 4:16

Take care of your health, that it may serve you to serve God.
–St Francis de Sales

We take excellent care of our bodies, which we have for only a lifetime; yet we let our souls shrivel, which we will have for eternity.
–Billy Graham

The soul, like the body, lives by what it feeds on.
–Josiah Holland

sign posts

what if?

What are the vital 'vitamins' we need for our Christian life? What is the Vitamin C of Christian nutrition?

What is the recommended daily dose of God?

How do we get more energy for God?

Which bits of your Christian life need nourishing?

Imagine if you could take Talent Tablets.

Do you take in Spiritual Body-Building Vitamins to pose on the beach of theology, or digest Spiritual Vitamins to develop your ministry's stamina in the cross-country event to raise funds for good works? Or have you passed out halfway through this sentence?

Eat your greens.

Go for a month without eating anything that comes out of plastic.

Feed the neglected parts of your Christian life.

Read, pray, go on courses, take your spiritual supplements.

When you go to the gym, spend your time on the treadmill praying. And not just for survival.

straight ahead

Convince yourself that scurvy is attractive.

Take your vitamins by intravenous injection instead.

'O Lord, *fooooooooooood!*... Amen!'

dRAINS

street life

Plip, plip, plip, plip, flluuussssh, fweeart, fwoosh, swlop, shplawsh, swlop, shplawsh, swlop, schwerl, schwelle, swlop, stench, pfwong, swlop, plip, plip, plip, plip.

street bible

Psalm 40:1-3

I waited, waited quiet, quite calm;
He turned towards me, grabbed my arm,
Pulled me up from the cesspool's hold,
Away from the filth, the mud, the cold.
He stood me firm on solid rock,
A place no one dare knock.
He taught me a brand-new song to sing,
Spot on for the only true King.
Many will hear; many will see and fear
And rely on awesome God making it here.

street wise

Life can be the pits. Times when you feel like your whole life is down the sewer. Times of rejection, of failure. Times when we feel there's no direction left to us but down.

Sometimes we despair. We stop believing that we can get out of the situation we're in. We're down the drain, just make the best of it. Don't try to climb out, just make yourself comfortable down in the mud.

No. Look up. Through the grille, the blue sky shines. The pavement is just a step away. So take the hand that's offered you. Realize that God leaves no one in the gutter. Everyone is lifted up by love.

And if we're not in the gutter? If we're strolling along the sunny street with fine lives and light steps? Look down. Be God to those in the gutter. His hands are your hands. Reach down and rescue. Bring people back to solid ground.

streetlights

Genesis 37:20; Jeremiah 38; Psalm 7:15, 103:4; Proverbs 26:27; Isaiah 38:17; Luke 10:30–37; Galatians 6:1; Philippians 3:7 (see the King James Version for the word Paul used)

sign posts

The love of our neighbour is the only door out of the dungeon of self.
–George MacDonald

It is impossible for that man to despair who remembers that his helper is omnipotent.
–Jeremy Taylor

The only cure for suffering is to face it head on, grasp it round the neck, and use it.
–Mary Craig

what if?

Where are you at the moment? In the gutter or on the pavement?

Do you know people around you who need lifting up?

Do you believe that situations can change? Do you believe that God can change things?

straight ahead

There are Christians being persecuted all around the world. Do whatever you can to lift them out.

Do the chores in your house that nobody else wants to do.

Don't wear white when reclaiming people out of the sewer.

way out!

If you see someone in need, look the other way.

Comfort yourself with the idea that anyone in trouble is probably being punished by God.

If you're pushing people down into the sewer, take the drain cover off first.

'O Lord, *hug?*... Amen!'

cHURCh

street life

Well, it used to be a church. Now it's a 'Pound For Everything' shop. So I go in, walk up to the bloke behind the counter and say, 'Can I have an uplifting sing-along, a stimulating sermon and a strong sense of community spirit, please? Here's a pound.' He looks at me blank. 'Or should that be three pounds, one for each item?' Still blank. I walk out pretending to be disgruntled, wondering if he'll get it. Worth a try!

street bible

1 Peter 2:9-10

> But not you guys. No, no, no. You are the select, royalty in the role of God's reps to the people, an outstanding nation of ambassadors for God. You live and breathe to profile and celebrate the one who picked you up out of your dark grovellings and stood you in his brilliant light. One time you had no national identity; now you've got the full complement of work visas and passports of God's Nation. Once you only had what you deserved; now God's giving you breaks you'd never have expected.

street wise

What do you imagine by the word 'church'? A big building with a pointy bit at one end? A grim, time-blackened chapel where a preacher waves a big leather-black book at you? A warehouse where the worship band thrashes out the songs at deafness-inducing decibels?

Rewind to early times. Church wasn't a building. No church buildings till around three hundred years after Jesus died and the Holy Spirit called in the first church meeting. Before that everyone just met in houses.

Church isn't built of brick and stone, but of people. So when you meet together, that's church. What matters in church is the people. What holds church together is not mortar but relationships (just as sticky till firmly set).

Which means that we have to take our relationships seriously. We have to get to know one another, talk to one another, challenge one another, shine a little prophecy into people's lives.

Matthew 16:18; Romans 12:4–8; 1 Corinthians 6:19, 14:26; Colossians 1:24

signposts

The Christian Church is the one organization in the world that exists purely for the benefit of non-members.

–William Temple

God never intended his Church to be a refrigerator in which to preserve perishable piety. He intended it to be an incubator in which to hatch converts.

–F. Lincicome

He goes to church as he goes to the bathroom, with the minimum of fuss and no explanation if he can help it.

–Ronald Blythe

What if your church building burned down tonight? Would you still have a church?

What is the church for?

What do you like about church? What do you hate?

Is your church a refrigerator or an incubator?

Try going to church expecting God to speak to you. You never know . . .

Next time you're at church speak to someone you don't know. Find out about them. Really listen.

Next time someone starts moaning about the church, turn to them and say, 'I hereby appoint thee a bishop. Now let's see if thou canst do a better job, matey.'

way out!

Dress up in a suit and tie whenever you go to church.

If anyone at church mentions God say, 'Oh I'm only here for the architecture. Have you seen our beautiful apse?'

Get out of church as soon after the service as you can. That way you won't have to talk to anyone.

Take the crossword with you. It'll give you something to do during the service.

'O Lord, *um* . . . Amen!'

RefUGEe

street life

Thing is, with everyone dressing so grungy, you really can't tell. I mean, is he an Eastern European refugee or an off-duty student doctor? It gets confusing if you don't know who's who. I wish there was a way of knowing who should and shouldn't be here. We need a tangible way of assessing it. Like, maybe . . . 'if they've got a pulse, then they should be on God's planet'?

Yes, something like that.

street bible

Matthew 25:31-36,41,45

'When I come back . . . I'll start separating people out: "sheep" on my right side, "goats" on the left.

'I'll say to the "sheep", "You're in God's good books: come forward, collect what's been waiting for you since before I made the planets. All this 'cos I feel I owe you – when I was starving, you made me meals. When I was thirsty, you poured me a drink. When I was a loner in the corner, you opened out the circle and brought me in. When my clothes weren't up to the job, you took me shopping on your Visa. When my health was bad, you nursed me back to strength. I was in my prison cell; you swallowed your pride and visited me."

'But the "goats" on the left will get the opposite treatment: "Get out of my sight. You're in the biggest hole you could imagine, and the hole's on fire, heating up for Satan and his cronies later."

'I'll say, "Truth is, the lowest of the low is someone like me! So whatever you didn't do for them, you didn't do for me."'*

street wise

We're all foreigners, you know. We're citizens of heaven, really. It's just we're living in temporary exile here on earth.

Ours is a religion of refugees, a faith of foreigners, and the Bible, of course, recognizes this. So we have no right to mistreat others or sneer at those who have fled from intolerable situations. We have to exercise compassion as well as judgement. No knee-jerk reactions; no simplistic slogans; no hatred of people whose only crime is to be strangers in a strange land.

Because we're all in their position. And if we treat people with contempt, then when we eventually go home we might have some explaining to do.

*For full version, see *the street bible*.

Exodus 22:21; Leviticus 24:22; Ruth (the whole thing); Psalm 137, 146:9; Ezekiel 22:29; Malachi 3:5; Luke 10:25–37; Ephesians 2:11–19; 1 Peter 2:11; Hebrews 13:1–3

sign posts

Our neighbour is one we love because he is like ourselves. The stranger is one we are taught to love precisely because he is not like ourselves.

–Jonathan Sacks

Many more people in the world are concerned about sports than human rights.

–Samuel P. Huntington

Charity is no substitute for justice withheld.

–St Augustine of Hippo

what if?

What would you do if asylum seekers moved into your street?

How do we tell real asylum seekers from false?

Is there a difference between someone who comes to the West to earn money for his family and one who comes because of persecution?

If Jesus' home territory was heaven, does that mean he was a refugee down here?

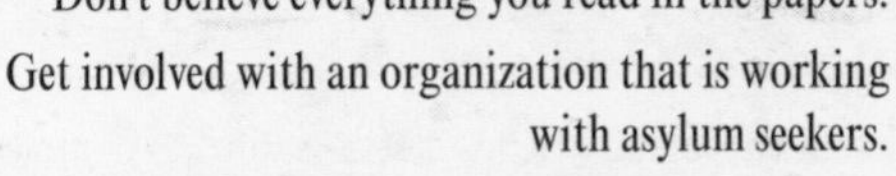

straight ahead

Find out the truth about the statistics.

Don't believe everything you read in the papers.

Get involved with an organization that is working with asylum seekers.

Write to the Foreign Office and ask them what they are doing about political and religious persecution.

way out!

They're all scroungers and they're only here to steal our jobs/benefits/women/garden tools, etc.

Ah, but it might *not* be an angel.*

Go out into your back yard. Put up a large sign saying 'Not in here'.

'O Lord, *who?*... Amen!'

*See Hebrews 13:2.

chocolate

street life

I mean, buying petrol is innocent enough. But it's always just there, within arm's reach. How many types of chocolate? And there's always a queue at the counter, making me stand there, just a grab away. Do they pay these people? Are they doing this on purpose? Don't they realize? Or is it just me who's tormented by the smell of the plastic wrappers? No, I must block out the wooing of the chocolate bars. But they call to me: 'You went jogging last night.' 'Eat me, just wear baggy jumpers.' 'Cover the spots with your mum's make up.' 'After the day you've had . . .' 'Go on, just this one.' But I must be strong. After all it's Easter soon, Lent will seem years back, and I've stockpiled those eggs for my nephews. They'll never know!

street bible

2 Corinthians 1:2-5

Major credit goes out to God, who's the father of our Boss, Jesus the Liberator, the God who loves you passionately and puts his arm around you, like a dad who understands. He's always there for us when it all goes pear-shaped, 'cos then we qualify to put our arm round someone else who's lost the plot. You're well clued up on the hassles of following Jesus – but as the struggle-stakes go through the roof, so do the stats for 'Comfort Received'.

street wise

We're in love with chocolate. Friends desert us, life lets us down, but chocolate – chocolate is always there for us. Chocolate is our favourite comfort food. (Well, chocolate and ice cream. Or better still, chocolate ice cream. With extra chocolate. And a flake stuck in it.)

We all need a refuge, a place of safety. Some eat chocolate, some relax in a nice warm bath. Some seek the comfort of family or friends. Yes, we all need a refuge, but not every refuge is safe. Seek shelter in drugs or alcohol and you might find the cure is worse than the disease.

A refuge should give you hope, not dull the pain of hopelessness. A refuge should protect and not ensnare.

So check out your hiding place. Tell God your troubles. Make him your place of shelter. Take refuge with God and he'll send you out stronger than before.

And while you're at it, get me a cream egg.

Psalm 2:12, 5:11, 9:9, 16:1, 17:7, 18:2, 31:2, 34:8, 36:7, 46:1, 62:8, 71:1, 91:2, 144:2 . . . er, you get the idea.

sign posts

God does not comfort us to make us comfortable, but to make us comforters. *–John Henry Jowett*

If we have no quiet in our minds, outward comfort will do no more for us than a golden slipper on a gouty foot. *–John Bunyan**

People who drink to drown their sorrow should be told that sorrow knows how to swim. *–Ann Landers*

Oh, the comfort, the inexpressible comfort of feeling safe with a person, having neither to weigh thoughts nor measure words, but pouring them all right out, just as they are . . . *–Dinah Mullock Craik*

what if?

In what do you take refuge?

In times of trouble how can God help us?

What if all the land in the Third World devoted to the cocoa plant was re-seeded with food crops?

Are Chocolate Hobnobs (a) a biscuit or (b) a disease or (c) both?

Which do you prefer, milk or plain?

If you finish off someone else's chocolate gateau, it's their calories, surely?

straight ahead

Check your own addictions. Are you eating too much chocolate? Drinking too much coffee? Smoking too many cigarettes?

Try fasting. Deliberately go without your favourite comfort food and spend the time with God instead.

Talk to trusted friends or family about your troubles. Let them help to carry your burdens.

Go and buy a large bar of Galaxy. Eat it all yourself.

Don't give up chocolate for Lent; give up Lent for chocolate.

'O Lord, *sugar!* . . . Amen!'

*Or, given the end of the quote, maybe that should be John Bunion.

SMOG

street life

You get used to it. Just go up closer if you want to read a road sign. Just stock up on lozenges for that sore throat that greets you when you wake up. Cover your skin with creams, exfoliators, moisturizers. But what you don't see is the internal damage, where you can't apply the lotions. What you don't know are the long-term effects. What you can't block out are the toxins that lock into your system and gradually strangle you. So what is the price of spiritual de-toxins to purify us from all the gunk we breath in from living in Spiritual Smog City?

street bible

Titus 1:15-16

> If you're pure, you see the pure in everything. If your conviction's been polluted, then everything's innuendo and smut. They've got three-track minds: filth, filth and more filth. They've had their conscience removed – it's in a jar on the shelf, curled up and comatosed. They spout off about how they and God are 'this close'. But their lifestyle gives them away – they've never even met him.

street wise

Walk through mud and you'll get dirty. Walk through smog and it's hard to breathe. Out on the streets our minds get dirty. Our souls get rained on. We see images that disturb; hear language that shocks; encounter people who make you feel . . . well, not holy, let's just say that.

How do we stay pure? Two choices:

1 Stay in – don't go out. Put a paper bag over your head.
2 Ask God to protect you as you wade through the world.

Number 2 seems best. Because we don't have the option of staying in our rooms. We're supposed to go out there and pull people from the mud. And you can't pull people from the mud without getting dirty; you can't rescue people from the sea without getting wet. And the truth is that it's only through his protection that we escape infection. Just trust in God. Plug into his purity, ask for his protection and, if the world creeps in, ask for his forgiveness and he'll wash you clean again.

Psalm 19:9, 24:4, 119:9; Proverbs 20:9, 20:30; Matthew 5:8; Philippians 4:8; 1 Thessalonians 5:23–24; 1 Timothy 5:22; Titus 1:15, 16; James 1:27; 1 Peter 1:22; 1 John 1:7–9

sign posts

Purity is the power to contemplate defilement.
–Simone Weil

Sanctify yourself and you will sanctify society.
–St Francis of Assisi

There is no single definition of holiness: there are dozens, hundreds. But there is one I am particularly fond of: being holy means getting up immediately every time you fall, with humility and joy. It doesn't mean never falling into sin. It means being able to say, 'Yes Lord. I have fallen a thousand times. But thanks to you I have got up again a thousand and one times.' That's all. I like thinking about that. – *Helder Camara*

what if?

What does it mean to be holy?

What is the difference between being 'holy' and being 'holier-than-thou'?

What kind of things make you impure?

Jesus said it is not what goes into a man that matters but what comes out. Does this mean it's OK to smoke providing you don't exhale?

Pray. Lots of times. Every day.

If you see something that you know has affected you, pray about it.

Keep out of temptation. Stay away from things that you know affect you. Turn off the TV, take another route, don't go near that shelf in the shops.

way out!

Argue that 'I'm mature enough not to be affected.'

When someone points out that you have spent ten minutes drooling at that picture of the pop stars in their underwear, reply that you're 'just appreciating the beauty of creation'.

'O Lord, *gasp* . . . Amen!'

NUGGETS

street life

I'm famished. But the whole day's running ahead of me and I've got so much to do. Fantastic, there's a BurgerMcKFCHut. No time to stop and enjoy the luxury and style of the award-winning interior décor. No, this'll be drive-thru. But the queue's back to the road . . . the last two orders took an average of two minutes eighteen seconds . . . and there's still nine cars and a moped between me and my large McSlurryNuggetWings!

street bible

Galatians 5:22-26

> But if God's Spirit is in charge, then this is you: you're loving, alive, vibrant, sparkling. You're calm; you walk into a room and friction walks out. You can handle delays; you're not pushy. You're generous with money, with time, with people. You're good and solid, always ready to help. You don't double-cross people; you don't use your fists in anger; you don't lose your rag – you're in control. You're never in trouble with the police. That's you! You're connected with the Liberator Jesus and you've murdered your dark side with its 'must have' attitude. Now that we're living with God's Spirit, let's get our heartbeat in rhythm with his. Let's not get cocky, competitive or jealous.

street wise

I want it now! I want my meal right now. I want my coffee to go. I want microwaveable pizza. I want to lose pounds overnight. I want my house transformed in a weekend, my garden made-over immediately, my meals cooked in twenty minutes maximum. I want email, instant messaging and a super-fast broadband connection. I want 38 Gigaflopz computers and digital instant-download cameras. I want ready-mix concrete and ready-to-wear clothes. I want interest-free credit, buy-today-pay-tomorrow drive-it-away deals. I want knee-jerk solutions and overnight success. I want instant gratification and consequence-free delight. I want the government to give me exactly what I want and the opposition to promise to give me what I want. I want a better standard of living by tomorrow and world peace by Friday at the latest. I don't want what's best for me. I don't want to wait. I don't want to do without. I don't want patience. Unless I can have it immediately!

Job (just flick through it for now); Psalm 40:1; Proverbs 14:29, 19:11; Ecclesiastes 7:8; Isaiah 26:3; Jeremiah 6:16; Matthew 18:26, 29; Romans 12:12; 1 Corinthians13:4; 2 Corinthians 6:6; Colossians 1:11; 1 Thessalonians 5:14; 1 Timothy 1:16; 2 Timothy 4:2; Hebrews 6:15

sign posts

Possess your soul with patience. *–John Dryden*

Patience serves as a protection against wrongs as clothes do against cold. *–Leonardo da Vinci*

All men commend patience, although few be willing to practise it. *–Thomas à Kempis*

what if?

Why is patience a virtue?

Do all good things come to those who wait? Or is this just something parents say to shut you up?

Does the early bird catch the worm? Or does it just get frostbite?

What if there was a society where they had to actually pick/kill their food, prepare it, cook it and then sit round together and eat it? They'd never get anything done!

Which part of the animal is a 'nugget' anyway?

When you want to buy something, wait thirty days. If you still think you need it, fine. If not, you probably didn't really need it in the first place.

Grow some plants. It teaches you patience.

Take a tortoise for a walk.

way out!

Buy shares in an indigestion tablet producer.

Buy a kebab, start eating it, run to the car, then break the speed limit through all the red lights while trying to stop the salad bits falling in your lap and phoning ahead to get your mum/mate/partner to have the microwave door already open 'cos it'll have gone cold by the time you get there.

'O Lord, *mmm!* . . . Amen!'

GOSSIP

street life

Me? A gossip?! You should've heard what the Davies girls were saying about him! Sipping my latte, trying not to eavesdrop . . . but failing. Too juicy! And they're louder than Kev on a night out. They're slagging off some guy called Phil. He's not got a good track record or something – stuff about violence (like Mike got done for last month) and dodgy deals (sounds like could be Phil Betson down Clifton Street). This Phil's getting a right roasting; the girls reckon that he's got it coming and there might even be a gun involved! This is serious! What do I do? I'm only telling you 'cos I'm worried . . . Which is when one of them says, 'So, you watching it tonight?'

Oh. *EastEnders*. Of course. I knew that!

street bible

James 3:1-2, 9-12

Guys, don't push yourself forward to be a life coach, 'cos there's a different set of rules applied to those who've told others where to go / what to do / how to be . . . much tougher. We all mess up in loads of ways. But if you never open your mouth and put your foot in it, then you're perfect. If you can control your mouth, then you've got it all sussed.

Our mouths sing worship songs to our Boss, our Father; then, over coffee, the same mouth slags off someone who's made with God's character built in. One minute: holyspeak. Next minute: a filth fountain. All with the same mouth?! Guys, we're out of line. Spa sources don't produce pure mineral water one minute and then putrid gunk the next. You can't get drinking water out of a sewer. It may all be on the same shelf, but apples and pears come off different trees!

street wise

I'll tell you a secret: we all love a good gossip, don't we?

Not that we always call it what it is, of course. Oh no, that's the great thing about gossip: you can disguise it so easily. You can call it 'sharing your concerns' or even 'passing on items for prayer'. And then, under the guise of a caring, sharing, concerned individual, we can satellite dish the dirt in great big scoops.

Trouble is, gossip is toxic. Handle it too much, and you get contaminated.

streetlights

Psalm 5:9, 34:13, 52:4, 139:4; Proverbs 10:19, 17:20; Isaiah 59:3; James 1:26

signposts

Gossip is vice enjoyed vicariously.
–Elbert Hubbard

Whoever gossips to you will gossip about you.
–Spanish proverb

I always prefer to believe the best of everybody; it saves so much trouble.
–Rudyard Kipling

Speak when you are angry and you will make the best speech you will ever regret.
–Ambrose Bierce

what if?

What if you didn't say the first thing that came into your head sometimes?

Why do you think that gossip is so destructive?

Have you ever been hurt by gossip? Or have you ever hurt others?

In what circumstances *should* you 'betray' a confidence?

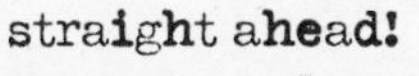

straight ahead!

Just stop gossiping. I mean, it's not rocket science, you know.*

Guard your tongue. Choose your words carefully. Refuse to handle explosive goods. (Psst. Pass this on to everyone you know.)

way out!

Claim you're from Yorkshire, then you're just speaking your mind.

It's OK if it's for prayer.

'O Lord, *oops!* . . . Amen!'

*This, however, is rocket science: $W = \int m \frac{dr}{dt} dv = \int mv.dv = \frac{1}{2} mv^2$

mobile

street life

I bought one of those programmable mobiles, the ones where you can sample in your own ring tone. Every time my phone goes off on the bus or somewhere, heads turn as the heavily reverbed voice booms out, 'This is God and I'm busting to tell you something!' Then, just to make the point, I stun the rest of the bus by not answering and carry on reading the sports page.

Or would God be so cool he'd mostly text? And if we ever got round to texting God back, would he be running the most advanced predictive texting software? Would he anticipate our every question, or would he wait for us to ask . . . and keep on asking . . . and keep on asking?

street bible

Psalm 139:1-6

God, you've picked me over and you know me, intricately;
You've sussed me out: you know me, intimately;
You forecast my every move: my body, brain, my big, big mouth!
You know all my tendencies, my habits, my times:
Before I've even said it, you've worked out if it rhymes;
Your armed guard stands round me, above me, below me;
You've put your arm around me: you know me;
My head doesn't have the capacity –
It's Overload City, this 'YOU and me'!

street wise

Funny, isn't it, how we're never out of contact with each other these days. Emails, phone calls, text messages – we talk and talk to each other, cramming the bandwidth with our every thought.

So, when was the last time you talked to God?

We have time for friends, clients, family, for the bloke we met in the pub last night, for the guy with the dyed blond hair who we danced with till dawn.

But for God? For the Being who spoke the first word? For the Creator who gave Moses all those messages texted on stone?

Nah. Put him on hold. Divert his calls. Wipe his number from your SIM.

Yet he's waiting to hear from you. And think about this: he's never out of signal range, his battery is never low, he's always listening.

Call him. Check your prayer-mail. No need to pay: your account is always topped up.

Deuteronomy 30:20; 1 Samuel 3:9; Nehemiah 8:3; Proverbs 12:15, 18:13; Isaiah 66:4; Ezekiel 2:5; Mark 9:7; Luke 10:39; John 10:27; James 1:19

Pray as you can and do not try to pray as you can't.
–John Chapman

Prayer is conversation with God. *–Clement of Alexandria*

Prayer enlarges the heart until it is capable of containing God's gift of himself. *–Mother Teresa*

A prayer in its simplest definition is merely a wish turned Godward. *–Phillips Brooks*

sign posts

what if?

Do you find prayer difficult? Why?

Does God keep leaving messages on your voice-mail?

What if we spent as much time praying as we do on the phone?

What makes you turn to prayer?

Have you ever considered writing up your prayers as a crafted piece of writing?

As you pray, imagine the outcomes of your prayers. Praying for healing for someone? Imagine them whole and well and walking around. Imagination gives your prayers more reality.

As you meet people today, send up an 'arrow' prayer for them. Ask that God will bless them. People on the bus, people at school, people at work – you don't have to know someone to pray for them.

Get together with friends and pray regularly together.

straight ahead

Don't give God your mobile number.

Use times of prayer as a good opportunity to text a few friends.

Since God reads your mind, there's no point really, is there?

Just string together a combination of religious jargan and Bible verses. God'll notice you're not praying , but no one else will.

'O Lord, *hello?* . . . Amen!'

SWINGS

street life

The alarm goes off. I slam my hand down before it wakes anyone. Creep out. Check the rest of the street. No one's up yet. It'll be completely empty, this is my chance! Get on my push bike, so silent. Nothing's going to give my game away. Glide down the street, still looking up at the net curtains – darkness reigns within. Arrive, sooo excited. Resist urge to scream with joy. Pad my way to the gate, slippers still on. Push the iron gate open – gently, they never oil these things. I'm in! Yesss! And it's all mine. I can hardly contain myself. Now which shall I play on first? The swings or the slide?

street bible

Matthew 18:1-4

Straight off the Team Twelve hit Jesus with a teaser, 'We're thinking Heaven On Earth, right?' Someone else chips in, 'Well, who's No. 1?' And another has his say, 'You know, in God's New World Order, who classifies as Numero Uno?' Now they're all getting in there, 'Top Dog', 'The Biggest Cheese', 'Biggest Noise', 'Biggest Shot', 'Biggest Toupee'?

Jesus signals for one of the local kids to come over and stand by him. And with this visual aid in front of him, he answers, 'On the level, unless you morph back into being kids again you won't even get your passport for Heaven On Earth. But to answer your question: whoever shifts into vulnerable, innocent, pure mode – whoever shifts and makes like this gem of a kid here – then you're talking "truly great" in God's New World Order.'

street wise

We know too much about the world these days. We've seen it all, explored everywhere; we know everything but believe in nothing. Cynicism makes us prematurely old; familiarity breeds indifference.

Jesus told us to be childlike, not childish. Not tantrum-throwing, pram-rattling toddlers, but children awed and excited by the world around them. To be childlike means that we can still enjoy the swings, the slides, climbing trees, that we're never too old to climb on to God's knee and listen while he tells us a story. The world is a great big box of treasure to be flung open and scattered around, not a secret bank account to be carefully invested and locked away.

Practise wonder. Open your eyes. It's a great world. And it looks even better from the swings.

Psalm 8:2; Matthew 11:25, 19:14; Mark 10:14–16; 1 Corinthians 13:11, 14:20

sign posts

Keep interested in others, keep interested in the wide and wonderful world. Then in a spiritual sense you will always be young.

–Fredric March

Wonder is the basis for worship.

–Thomas Carlyle

To be surprised, to wonder, is to begin to understand.

–Jose Ortega y Gasset

Wonder is especially proper to childhood, and it is the sense of wonder above all that keeps us young.

–Gerald Vann

what if?

If people said, 'You're acting like a child,' would you take it as a compliment?

Are there things you would like to do, but don't because you're supposed to be grown up?

What's the difference between being childlike and being childish?

Is it my turn on the see-saw yet?

Have you ever read *Sophie's World?**

straight ahead

Go for a slow walk with a toddler. Everything is amazing to them. A stone is a marvel, moss on a wall is a mystery.

Climb a tree.

Tell a story.

Never tell a child to grow up.

way out!

Just tut a lot.

Botox your face into a permanent frown, in case you forget yourself when something funny happens.

Oh, for heaven's sake, just grow up.

'O Lord, *WOW!* . . . Amen!'

*By Jostein Gaarder. It's about the history of philosophy, but don't let that put you off.

TRUANt

street life

How does he expect to get away with it? School uniform in the shopping precinct at 11am! Should I report him? I decide to confront him and ask him why he's wasting his life. He says, 'Do you have a minute to answer a questionnaire for my social studies project, sir? It's about preconceived ideas of teenagers by the older generation.'

street bible

Matthew 25:14-30

[A millionaire's off on a long business trip. He gets three of his staff to look after the dosh while he's away. One guy (a real talent) gets 500 grand; the second guy (good, but nothing stunning) gets 200 grand, and the last guy (steady) gets 'just' 100 grand. Then the boss is gone. The first guy invests, doubles his money. The second guy does the same. But the third guy bottles, buries the money. The boss comes back, and he's well impressed with Guy 1.]

'"Well done; done well! You've proved yourself, now you get to manage bigger projects for me. You and me, we've got good times lined up!"

'The second guy, also looking pleased with himself, says, "You gave me 200 grand, and I've doubled your money as well." Handing the boss the case, he says, "There's 400 grand in there." Likewise, his boss is impressed: "Well done; done well! I've got some good projects for you too. You'll have nothing to worry about from now on."

'[But then it's Guy 3, with the same old briefcase . . .] "You lily-livered, useless, gutless, spineless excuse for a half-life. You're pathetic . . . !"

'Then he takes the briefcase and gives it to the first guy saying, "You have it, 'cos those who've got loads, get given even more; and those who've got zilch, even what they've got'll get given to those with loads. That's how it works! And get this loser out of my sight! Throw him out on to the streets where he belongs. If he gets piles from the pavement, tough."'*

street wise

The trouble with learning about God is that we make it so boring. It's a tragedy because we're supposed to be investigators, explorers, discoverers of truth. Be a lifelong learner about God. There's so much to learn. God is a river that never runs dry, a land that stretches in all directions, a subject that can never be exhausted.

*For full version, see *the street bible*.

Proverbs 1:5, 6:6, 6:10, 9:9, 13:4, 20:4, 26:15; Colossians 2:6, 7

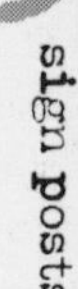

Anyone who stops learning is old, whether at twenty or eighty. Anyone who keeps learning stays young. The greatest thing in life is to keep your mind young. *–Henry Ford*

A teacher affects eternity; he can never tell where his influence stops. *–Henry Adams*

what if?

If you're at school or college, what are you learning that you could use to serve God?

What if you started reading the Bible tomorrow? What difference would it make?

Do we ever discover new things about God? Or do we rediscover old truths?

How did Jesus teach people? Why did he tell stories?

If you are a teacher, what other methods could you use to get your lessons across?

What if all your teachers had been awful, when would you have taken responsibility for your own study?

Which teacher would you most like to thank?

Identify the areas of your life where you need to learn some new skills.

Read the Bible. Start exploring.

Track down that great teacher and write him a letter.*

Sign up for an evening class . . . and go! . . . more than twice!

way out!

Buy a Sink-Into Sofa and a widescreen TV and see if you feel led to study.

Convince yourself that you're not clever enough / too old to learn anything new.

Don't read the book. Wait for the film to come out. Or better still, the T-shirt.

'O Lord, *help!* . . . Amen!'

*Make sure you check your spelling.

LIP GLOSS

street life

She stands there, trying every product on the counter. Crimsons, pinks, purples. Lip gloss, blusher, eye-liner. Nothing tested on animals, everything plastered on humans.

Is she happy, this girl? What is she looking for? Beauticians make the outside look great, but who will beautify the inside? Who will help us makeover the face we hide away from the world?

street bible

Matthew 23:26

Like I said before, you scrub the bowls and cups so they're sparkling on the outside, but on the inside you leave the bacteria of greed and selfishness to fester . . .

2 Corinthians 3:16-18

But when we turn our lives back towards the Boss, the mask is taken off. The Boss is the Spirit of God, and wherever God's Spirit is, there's freedom. We've got our masks off and God's brilliance is bouncing off our faces; it's changing us – our features are evolving; we're looking more and more attractive as God's Spirit puts plastic surgeons out of work by the thousands. Only our Boss makes us truly beautiful.

street wise

They haven't seen each other for years. Childhood sweethearts, their passion reignited via Friends Reunited. But does she really love him? Will she love him as he looks today? One way to test her devotion. Give the spray of lilies to a rough looking tramp and ask him to go up to her. He watches, she sees the street dweller approach and – yes! She runs towards him and kisses him. Proof!

What you look like is not who you are. True love looks beyond the appearances; real beauty shines out from the inside.

So plaster this on and let it soak in: the love of God is guaranteed. He loves you not for what you look like, but for who you are. He doesn't care about split ends, but about whole lives; he doesn't care about lipstick, but about whether those lips stick to the truth.

It's not a bad thing to use make up. But it's an even better thing to make up with God. Wear his forgiveness and love and you'll always be beautiful.

1 Samuel 16:7; Esther 2:1–9; Proverbs 5:3–14, 11:22; Isaiah 53:2; Ezekiel 16:15, 28:17; Matthew 23:26–27; Titus 3, 6–8; 1 Peter 3:3–6

sign posts

I'm tired of all this nonsense about beauty being only skin-deep. That's deep enough. What do you want, an adorable pancreas? *–Jean Kerr*

No man, for any considerable period, can wear one face to himself and another to the multitude, without finally getting bewildered as to which may be the true. *–Nathaniel Hawthorne*

God's fingers can touch nothing but to mould it into loveliness. *–George MacDonald*

what if?

Do you ever pretend to be someone you're not?

What does it mean to say that 'God looks at the heart'?

Is Christianity just a lip gloss that you put on on Sunday? Or is it something real, inside you?

What is lip gloss actually for? Wouldn't it be cheaper just to dribble a lot?

straight ahead

Don't pretend. Don't lie. Let your actions try to echo your beliefs.

Don't judge people on their appearance. Try to look a little deeper.

Be prepared to be vulnerable and open to people. Your vulnerability will let God shine through.

Think before you give your lilies to a tramp. He might run off with your girlfriend.

way out!

Learn how to fake sincerity.

Don't ever reveal your true feelings to others.

When people ask you 'How are you?' always say, 'Fine.'

If in doubt, look holy.

'O Lord, *thanks!* . . . Amen!'

CAR STEREO

street life

I'm sitting there waiting for the lights to turn green. The only thing helping me pass the time is the CD in my disc changer, when I can't even hear myself be impatient 'cos some boy racer has pulled up in his mobile stadium-spec PA system on wheels. My thoughts scream over the noise; 'No way's he converting me to thrashfusiondrum'n'bassmetal!' And, defiantly, I crank my Kenwood up to 'hi'. Let's see how he copes with Engelbert Humperdink at full volume!

street bible

Mark 4:33-34

> With loads of stories and images Jesus teaches them about God's ways. He feeds them as much as they can take in without giving them indigestion. He says nothing to them without using an image, picture or symbol of some sort to get through. But when he's 'backstage' with his team, he explains everything.

street wise

I was speaking to a Venezuelan friend of mine about the differences between his country and mine. He surprised me. It wasn't the health service or the standard of living or the politics, it was the conversation. 'In Venezuela,' he said, 'conversation is like a rope tied between us. I pull you one way and you respond. You pull me back. But here there is no rope between us. Here, it is like a wall and we just shout over the top at each other.'

Which just about sums up a lot of evangelism. We lob tracts and videos over the top of the wall. No connection between us and those we are trying to contact. Just a big wall between us. Or we drive very fast down their street with the radio on full blast, hoping that, despite our speed, they'll catch a few words and suddenly join us in the car park. No thought of stopping the car and getting out. That might mean we have to talk to them.

Jesus walked among us. He didn't zoom by on a cloud followed by some fast-moving cherubim churning out a drum 'n' bass version of the Hallelujah Chorus. He made friends. He made connections. He pulled people towards him.

He still does. But sometimes we have to help them hold the rope.

2 Samuel 12:1–10; Matthew 12:34; 1 Corinthians 2:1–5; 2 Timothy 2:23–26; Titus 3:9–11

sign posts

The wind and the sun had a competition to see who could get the man to take his coat off. The wind went first: blowing and gusting and busting a gut, but all that happened was that the man pulled his coat even closer into himself. The wind went off in a huff. The sun took his turn: glowing and sizzling and frizzling, and the man got all hot and can't be bothered and took his coat off voluntarily.

–Traditional fable

what if?

Does our evangelism seem a little intrusive at times?

What if we only gave answers when we're asked questions?

Did you realize that the Bible is roughly 53% story, 29% poetry, 18% teaching? Discuss!

Would Jesus be kicked out fo Evangelism Training for not being direct enough?

Join our society of Reluctant Evangelists – pretending that we don't want to talk about it much and drawing them into probing further – it's amazing how well it all works when you don't try so hard.

Instead of preaching it, put it into a story form. Let them work out what it means. Intrigue them. Jesus did.

Read up so you're ready when they *do* ask.

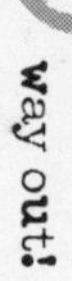

way out!

Keep shouting at them till they beg you to tell them your testimony.

Drive down the road very fast shouting, 'Jesus loves you, you unrepentant sinners!'

'O Lord, *how?*. . . Amen!'

CABLES

street life

Rip up the pavement, pull up the floorboards and hide them away. Run them behind the sofa. Plaster them into the walls. We must not have them taking the credit for all we do. We must not be seen to be needing their supplies. We must show that we are all-powerful and not dependent upon mere plastic-coated wires. No, we will continue with our dream of omnipotence, we will not bow to the source, we will not give away our glory to another. Never! Never! Nev – hang on, the lights have just fused.

street bible

Colossians 1:9-14

So, from day one of hearing your story we've been pushing your case with God, asking him to fill you in on his plans via his spiritual wisdom package. Why? So your lifestyle will ring true. So they'll look at you and it'll be obvious you belong to the Boss. So you'll make God happy in every category of life – getting on with good things, getting to know him personally because you're plugged into his power supply which is dazzling, long lasting, the only high worth having. So you'll be bubbling with joy – and you'll know who to credit: the one who's signed you in for a chunk of inheritance (tax free). So you'll twig that the son he loves has paid up front (in blood) for you to be dragged over the border from the Dark Nation into his Light Country with your slate wiped clean.

street wise

Whatever you do, you need power to do it. Electricity, gas, petrol, porridge* – whatever powers you on your journey through life.

Mostly, we hide those sources of power away. Pretend we're operating in our power. Kings of Creation. Masters of the Universe. But then it only takes a power cut and the whole place goes to pieces.

With God's power it's a different kettle of fish. (Although why you would put fish in a kettle is beyond me. Unless you like kipper-flavoured Darjeeling.)

Christians need God's power. Without the Holy Spirit in our lives what can we achieve? Can electricity make us love one another? Can petrol bring peace? Can porridge make us more forgiving? (Almost definitely not.) Only God's power gives us the ability to live the way he wants. And only by constantly plugging into his power will we get the energy we need to shine a light in this world of ours.

*The German word for porridge is *hafferschleim*. Literally, 'wheat slime'. We just thought you ought to know.

streetlights

2 Chronicles 32:7; Job 9:4; Psalm 66:3, 145:6; Isaiah 40:10; Zechariah 4:6; Matthew 22:29; Luke 1:35; Acts 1:8; Romans 1:20; 1 Corinthians 1:17; 2 Corinthians 4:7, 13:4; Ephesians 1:19, 3:14–21; 2 Timothy 3:5

sign posts

Those who have the gale of the Holy Spirit go forward even in sleep. *–Brother Lawrence*

There is one source of power that is stronger than every disappointment, bitterness or ingrained mistrust, and that power is Jesus Christ, who brought forgiveness and reconciliation to the world. *–Pope John Paul II*

We are the wire, God is the current. Our only power is to let the current pass through us. *–Carlo Carretto*

what if?

What if you didn't have the power of the Holy Spirit in your life? What difference would it make?

Why did God send the Holy Spirit? Isn't our own strength enough?

How do you plug into God's power each day?

The next time you're in a tough situation, ask God to plug you into his power.

Spend some time reading the Bible, praying.

Look at other ways of recharging your spiritual batteries, like going on a retreat or praying with friends.

way out!

Don't listen to God. Tell yourself you're conserving spiritual energy.

Pull the plug out.

Claim you've blown a fuse.

'O Lord, *yours!* . . . Amen!'

sex shop

street life

There's something weird going on in our high street: Broken Toys R Us has just opened up right next door to Dodgy Electricals, which is down from Furry Vegetables and across from Putrid Bakery. Piles of these twisted, spoiled goods can all be bought with money from a cashpoint that only issues counterfeit notes. Seems like the sex shop approach to selling warped versions of original wholesome products is really catching on. Should I campaign?

street bible

Proverbs 5:3-6

A woman with no morals may have chocolate-flavoured lipstick. She may have a voice that pulls you in like a magnet. But after it all, what've you got? A bad taste in your mouth from the rusty razor blade she slipped you mid-snog. She'll mince her way down to death, lead you to your very own grave on the way. She's got no idea where the road to life is – she missed it miles back and she's too dumb to turn around.

Don't look back and regret your lifelong service to your hormones. Learn from others' mistakes, not your own. Get up close and personal with your husband or wife. Full stop.

1 Corinthians 6:18-19

Sort your sex lives. All the rest of your mess doesn't get into your bones like a dodgy sex life does. It eats away at you like nothing else. Haven't you caught on? Your body is God's new HQ. His Holy Spirit lives in you, permanent contract. You don't own you anymore.

street wise

There are drugs that we don't think are drugs. There are dangerous substances out there that we don't think are doing us any harm at all. So we carry on using them, unaware that with each dose we're being pulled further into addiction and further from reality.

Pornography is addictive. It might start innocently enough, but before long we're craving harder and harder versions. It treats people as objects. It ruins and destroys people. It takes something that God intended to be part of a relationship and sells it on the street corner. It takes what should be an intimate, private delight and splashes it in the open for everyone to gaze at.

Porn is not only cheap, it's cheapening.

Genesis 1:23–25, 46:10; 2 Samuel 11; Song of Songs; Ezekiel 16:1–63; Luke 15:13, 30; John 8:1–11

sign posts

About sex especially men are born unbalanced,
we might almost say men are born mad.
They scarcely reach sanity till they reach sanctity.
–G. K. Chesterton

Sex has become one of the most discussed subjects of modern times. The Victorians pretended it did not exist; the moderns pretend that nothing else exists.
–Fulton J. Sheen

Pornography is of no use to me. I don't even have a pornograph to play it on.
–David McKay

what if?

Does God think sex is dirty?

Why does it matter if you just sleep with someone?*

Britain has the highest rate of teenage pregnancy in Europe. Why do you think this is?

Can 'porn' also be spelt 'pawn'?

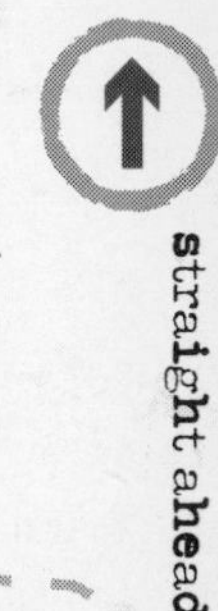

straight ahead

Write to your local council, just don't sound like Mrs Huffity from Pompous Towers.

Junk all that spam mail.

Think about what you wear. Are you wearing stuff that you know will arouse people?

Don't linger in the newsagent's, looking at things you know you shouldn't.

Just make sure no one sees you. If they do, tell them *again* that you're just appreciating the beauty of creation, so just back off. (See Smog, p. 56.)

'O Lord, *yuk!* . . . Amen!'

*Actually, the problem is more to do with staying awake with somebody, but you know what we mean.

SCAFFOLDING

street life

You wonder whether they used to play with Meccano when they were just chubby little boys. You wonder whether they begged their dads to build them tree houses. You wonder whether their favourite superhero was always, unquestionably, Spiderman. Now they're grown men with muscles on their muscles, you wonder if they ever have dreams where they fall off their own scaffolding. You wonder how brave or blasé they are about being right up there on a wooden plank just to build us a new office block. You wonder if they deliberately buy jeans three sizes too big. You wonder if they wonder. Rare.

street bible

Matthew 7:24-27

Jesus rounds off the Sermon on the Mount with, 'So, anyone who takes all this in and applies it, turns it into a lifestyle – they're like the guys from "In The Know Construction Co" who know their geology and only build on solid rock. The rain sheets down, the place is declared a flood disaster area, gale force winds and worse rattle through the girders. But it stays standing 'cos it's built on solid rock.

'But anyone who hears all this and does nothing to change their lifestyle – they're like the cowboys from "Dumb and Sons Builders", who buy up cheap land that's not even sandstone, just sand – and do the construction work with fingers crossed. Same rain sheets down, same flood alert, same gale force winds. End result? Mangled girders and shattered bricks.'

street wise

What kind of life-builder are you?

When it comes to constructing your own life do you check out the plans, look at God's building regulations and build on solid ground? Or are you a cowboy-builder, using cheap materials, cutting corners, hoping that the quick-drying plaster will cover the cracks?

God builds things to last. Not temporary accommodation, but lives that will last for eternity. To do that we have to use his materials of truth and love and build on his foundations. 'Whoever wants to save his life will lose it; lay down your own life for your friends' – strange health and safety rules, if you ask me, but he's the Boss.

So whose plans will you follow? Who's the architect of your life? You or God?

Psalm 127:1; Proverbs 3:5–6; Isaiah 55:8, 9;
1 Corinthians 3:10–17; Ephesians 4:12; 1 Peter 2:5

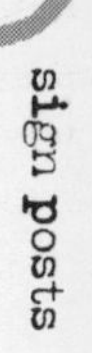

Every man is the architect of his own fortune.
–Appius Claudius

In my experience, if you have to keep the lavatory door shut by extending your left leg, it's modern architecture.
–Nancy Banks Smith

In spite of everything I still believe that people are really good at heart. I simply can't build up my hopes on a foundation consisting of confusion, misery and death.
–Anne Frank

what if?

What are the foundations in your life? What are the values that keep your life stable and secure?

If your life were a building what kind would it be? A house? A church? A shop? An igloo?

What kinds of things threaten the building of your life? What can you do about them?

Is your life strong enough to stand up to the storms?

If you had an architect's instructions would you still use those old sheets of corrugated iron for your extension?

Write down your core values – the things that make your life stable and secure.

Draw a picture of the building that is your life. Or make one out of Lego. What does it look like?

Build your house with straw and swear that the big bad wolves don't get huffity these days.

Ignore the survey report that says the bargain house you're about to buy is built on quicksand.

'O Lord, *d'oh!* . . . Amen!'

CASHPOINT

street life

Sat in the coffee house and watched people at the cashpoint machine. Before long I was playing the 'Guess the Balance' game. It's not hard. First, check general body language. Second, time the transaction. If it takes longer than thirty-eight seconds, they're checking their balance and the game is on! Moving into the Walk Away section of the game, you must focus hard. Has the angle of neck dropped (indicates Worse Than Expected balance)? Has their stride lengthened (indicates Better Than Expected balance)? Are they smiling/frowning/fainting/singing worship songs? Then make your guess: 'Better' or 'Worse'. If you picked 'Worse' and they go into a charity shop – congratulations, you win this round. If you picked 'Worse' and they head straight for a designer label zone – you lose.

street bible

Matthew 6:19-21, 24

Jesus says, 'Don't spend your life stockpiling goods with a sell-by date. Don't invest in yesterday's technology. Don't put your money into stuff that can just get nicked. Build up your balance in heaven's bank vaults, where nothing rots, where nothing dates, where nothing gets nicked. Want to know where a guy's heart is? Track down where he invests his stash and his heart won't be more than an arm's length away.

'No one can do two full-time jobs. They'll either be well into the first and resent having to turn up for the second, or they'll hate the thought of the first and look forward to clocking on for the second. You can't work for both God and materialism.'

street wise

'You are what you earn'. That's the message posted today; that's the banner hanging across the high street. You're not anyone unless you've got the cash.

Don't think so, actually. Surely you are who you worship.

That's why Jesus talked about the impossibility of serving two masters. Make Jesus your God and you'll be every day trying to be like him: more loving, more forgiving, more kind. Make money your god and you'll be like that instead. You'll be like a coin: hard, glittery, uncaring.

We all need money to live, wages to survive. But how much? There's a difference between seeing money as a necessity of life and seeing money as life itself.

Deuteronomy 8:18, 14:22; 2 Chronicles 1:11; Psalm 39:6; Proverbs 3:9–10, 10:4, 11:4, 13:11, 15:16, 18:11, 22:4; Ecclesiastes 5:10–13; Song of Songs 8:7; Matthew 13:22; Mark 10: 17–31; Luke 15:13, 19:10f; Acts 5:2; 1 Timothy 3:3, 6:17; 2 Timothy 3:2; Hebrews 13:5; James 5:1–3; 1 Peter 5:2

sign posts

Money has never yet made anyone rich. *–Seneca*

Make all you can, save all you can, give all you can. *–John Wesley*

The real measure of our wealth is how much we'd be worth if we lost all our money. *–John Henry Jowett*

A person will worship something, have no doubt about that. We may think our tribute is paid in secret in the dark recesses of our hearts, but it will out. That which dominates our imaginations and our thoughts will determine our lives, and our character. Therefore, it behoves us to be careful what we worship, for what we are worshipping we are becoming. *–Ralph Waldo Emerson*

what if?

Is it wrong to be rich?

What if Jesus told you to give all your money to the poor today? Could you do it?

If there was an option on your local cashpoint to check either your earthly or your heavenly bank balance, which would you go to first?

Should we pray for Lottery wins for our friends?

If you pay tax, set up a charity account with CAF* – get the tax man chipping in too!

Find out where your money goes. Keep a record of all you spend for one week, then ask yourself if you're spending money on the right things

Use the 'I give God my time instead' argument.

Write 'God helps those who help themselves' in your Bible in crayon. If anyone asks, claim it's one of Solomon's lost proverbs.

'O Lord, *where?*... Amen!'

*Not the Catfish Adoration Foundation – check out www.cafonline.org.

TRAFFIC LIGHTS

street life

They say the two hardest things in life are starting and finishing. But then waiting is pretty challenging too. We're revving away looking at the lights waiting for them to turn amber, in first gear ready to gain that oh-so-crucial five metres. Hard as this is, at least we've got the little man in the traffic light telling us when to stop and when to go. But with relationships, careers, lifestyle choices, we have to decide for ourselves when to pull off from stationary, when to slam on the brakes and come to a standstill. There is no man . . . or is there?

street bible

Joshua 1:6-9

'So I want you gutsy and going for it, 'cos I'm going to give you the land deeds I promised your grandparents. No room for getting the frighteners on. You've got to have guts and bottle to stick to the Big Ten I dictated to Moses. Don't add provisos or conditions, subclauses or cop-outs. Stick to them and you'll see success – big time. Chew over Moses' Rule Book like it's gum (it won't lose its flavour). Mull it over all day, dream about it all night – marinate your brain in it. It should be a reflex, a natural-born instinct to live right, like the book says. 'Cos then you'll all do well, you'll succeed, you'll live long and prosper. This isn't a suggestion; it's an instruction, an order, a Head Office Directive – go for it, full on, large. Now's not the time for wimps, losers or lard-hearts, 'cos the big-guy-in-the-sky goes with you wherever you go. Got it? Then DO it!'

street wise

Human being. That's what you are, you who are reading this: you're a human being.*

Funny name that is. Because if there's one thing humans aren't very good at, it's just 'being'. We're better at living in the past – 'human been' perhaps – dwelling on past mistakes or long-gone glories. We're even better at being 'human will be's' – looking into the future, dreaming dreams, planning what we will do when everything comes right.

But as for just 'being', as for just living in the here and now? Nope. I can't just be, I've too much to do.

Fact is, we can't tell what the future will bring. Oh, we make our plans, but God's in charge, and he might have a very different direction for us to go.

*Well, you could be a very, very intelligent dog, but we think that's unlikely.

Genesis 12:1; Joshua 1:6–9; Psalms 27:14, 130:5; Proverbs 16:9, 21:30; Isaiah 1:16, 30:18; Jeremiah 32:40; Matthew 25:1–46; Romans 8:23

sign posts

He who neglects the present moment throws away all he has. *–Johann von Schiller*

We are always getting ready to live but never living. *–Ralph Waldo Emerson*

The Procrastinator's Creed:
1 I believe that if anything is worth doing, it would have been done already.
2 I shall never move quickly, except to avoid more work or find excuses. *–Anon*

Take time to deliberate, but when the time for action arrives, stop thinking and go in. *–Andrew Jackson*

what if?

What would you say if God told you to go to another town, or even another country? Would you be ready to go?

Is it possible to do the right thing at the wrong time?*

What kinds of things should Christians be ready for?

If Christ came back tomorrow, would you be asking him for a few minutes more?

If you take off the 'shoes fitted with readiness that comes from the gospel of peace' (Ephesians 6:15) what do your feet stink of?

Be alert for opportunities to serve God.

Have your engine running in case God turns the traffic light green.

Don't just rush into things and hope for the best. Draw up plans. God really doesn't mind organized people.

Top up your petrol tank before it hits 'E'.

Just hope for the best.

Drive through every red light, see how ahead of schedule you get.

'Oh Lord, *yes?*... Amen!'

*Come to think of it, is it possible to do the right thing the wrong way up? Or even back to front?

SATELLITE DISH

street life

I've sussed it. Daytime telly is a government scheme to get people out of the house and looking for work. I was off work for yonks and old Dead Eye in the corner nearly pushed me to the limit. And having a satellite dish doesn't help, it just gives the thumb on your remote control hand some exercise. CLICK '. . . and the crowd's gone quiet waiting for . . .' CLICK '. . . a report just out says we're a nation of . . .' CLICK '. . . succulent tomatoes ready for sending to . . .' CLICK '. . . punk that took a bullet in the arm . . .' CLICK '. . . over to our correspondent who's speaking to . . .' CLICK '. . . a skateboarding duck . . .' CLICK.

If only it made this much sense!

street bible

Matthew 6: 22-23

'Your eyes are the windows to your soul. If your eyes are kept clean and healthy, loads of light will get into your soul. But if your eyes are all clogged up with gunk from the streets there'll be no light bouncing on to your soul. And if even your soul's shrivelled up from light-deprivation, then how dark is that?

Philippians 4:8-9

To round off, guys: stuff your mouth with truth; pack your head with heroic ideas; occupy your hands with doing the right thing; stack up your deep places with purity; focus your vision on beautiful things; fill your imagination with excellence, dignity, distinction. Copy me. Whatever you picked up from my words or mannerisms – work it into your lifestyle, and the God of serenity will hang around you.

street wise

Let's be straight; there's good and bad. But the issue is how much of it we consume. How much the TV fills our mind with junk.

There's this thing, this zombification of society, that happens when we just see too much. See too much violence, you're not shocked by it any more. See too much sex and you lose the mystery. See too much suffering and you lose the ability to respond.

But then there are the good things. Great films, life-enhancing comedy, stuff that moves us to anger, stuff that shakes us out of complacency.

Job 31:1; Psalm 119:37; Proverbs 17:24; Matthew 5:29; 2 Corinthians 4:18; Hebrews 12:2

sign posts

You know the great thing about television? If anything important happens, anywhere in the world . . . you can always change the channel.
–Jim Ignakowsky

Television's message has always been that the need for truth, wisdom and world peace pales by comparison with the need for a toothpaste that offers whiter teeth and fresher breath. *–Dave Barry*

Moral passion without entertainment is propaganda, and entertainment without moral passion is television.
–Rita Mae Brown

what if?

What if nothing much happened one day? How would the 24-hour-news stations fill their time?

What would happen to your life if you didn't watch TV for a week? What would you talk about?

Why are American TV presenters that strange colour?

What's on the other side?

What if the TV colour went dodgy and it was *white* people dying on our screens?

What did they do in the evenings a hundred years ago? So how come we're more bored than they were?

Turn off the TV. Do it now.

Go on a TV fast. Spend a week without watching the box. Spend the time reading your Bible, praying, talking to friends, whatever . . .

Whatever you watch, ask questions. What is this really saying? What values are celebrated by this programme? What can I learn from this?

Pass me the remote control, I think there's some wrestling on.

'O Lord, *downloading* . . . Amen!'

GUm

street life

Is she chewing that because she's just such a cool chick with attitude? Or does she have bad breath from a curry last night? Even less alluring when she gobs it out and it's now stuck to the sole of my shoe. I'm crouched down working spaghetti strings of sticky confectionery out of the chunky tread of my Docs with a bit of old stick. Is it me or does this smell of stale curry? Urgh!

street bible

Psalm 51:1-2, 10-13

Mercy me; God, mercy me, in line with your limitless love,
In line with your passion for me, wipe out my mess;
Wash off my filth; clean up my life. Mercy me; yeah, mercy me.
But my heart needs a transplant –
A fresh, clean heart, never used before today,
A gleaming, pure heart and a boost of resolve to keep it that way.
Don't banish me: I need to be right next to you;
Don't punish me; don't take away your Spirit too!
Give me back the buzz at being yours,
Then I'll take them all around on tours;
I'll say, 'Stick everything else on pause;
Put everything you've got behind this cause.'

street wise

They always used to say that 'mud sticks'. But it doesn't. You can wash mud off. Chewing gum, that's a different matter. Chewing gum, you need a combination of industrial-strength solvents, a large scrubbing brush and a sand-blasting device.

The world can throw these things at you, stuff that makes it difficult to walk with God because you keep sticking to the pavement.

Don't know what it is; different things stick to different people. Some people don't walk as smooth as they can because of greed. Other people are slowed down by ambition, or lust, or hatred. For some it's the past, a burden of hatred and resentment they carry with them through their lives.

So sometimes you have to let God make you clean. You have to own up to the things that you're clinging to – and which are clinging to you and let God clean the stuff off your shoes. (Don't worry – he's really into cleaning feet.)

Then, forgiven, released, de-gummed, you can go forward with him, not stuck down and limping along, but striding out in hope and purpose.

Leviticus 16:30; 1 Kings 8:39; Psalms 130:4; Proverbs 5:22,23; Ezekiel 33:10; Matthew 6:12; Mark 2:7; Galatians 6:1; Ephesians 1:7; Hebrews 12:1, 9:22; James 5:16; 1 John 1:9

sign posts

For him who confesses, shams are over
and realities have begun. *–William James*

Forgiveness is the answer to the child's dream
of a miracle by which what is broken is made whole again,
what is soiled is made clean again. *–Dag Hammarskjold*

God has cast our confessed sins into the depths of the sea,
and he's even put a 'No Fishing' sign over the spot.
–Dwight L. Moody

Forgiveness does not change the past,
but it does enlarge the future. *–Paul Boese*

what if?

Is there a solvent to remove sin from your life?

What if people could see your thoughts? Would they be X-rated?

Why is 'sin' such a taboo word today?

straight ahead

Ask God for his forgiveness.

Don't feel forgiven? Pray with someone else. Share your difficulties with them. You don't need them to forgive you, but sometimes it helps to hear it from another person.

Write down your failings and problems on a piece of paper. Put them in an envelope and post them to: God, Forgiveness Centre, Heaven. Don't put a return address. They're gone now.*

Put your gum in the bin provided.

way out!

Say to yourself, 'It's not a sin if no one knows about it.'

Convince yourself Moses came down from the mountain with Ten Suggestions.

Try to find the phrase 'A little of what you fancy does you good' in Deuteronomy.

'O Lord, *sorry* . . . Amen!'

*Or you could just burn them, which would help the postman a bit.

trees

street life

Trees . . . nice, aren't they? What would we do in a world without trees? Well, suffocate, obviously. Amazing when you think about it. Towns and cities are full of these big, green life-support machines. And we hardly notice them, except to carve our names in them. I'd really miss trees. Although probably not as much as my dog would . . .

street bible

Genesis 1:9-13

Day three: God says, 'Too much water! We need something to walk on, a huge lump of it – call it "land". Let the "sea" lick its edges.' God smiles, says, 'Now we've got us some definition. But it's too plain! It needs colour! Vegetation! Loads of it. A million shades. Now!' And the earth goes wild with trees, bushes, plants, flowers and fungi. 'Now give it a growth permit.' Seeds appear in every one. 'Yesss!' says God.

Genesis 2:8-9

God places the guy in the special garden he's planted, called 'Eden'. God's planted loads of types of trees in the garden – they look great and their fruit tastes great. Smack bang in the middle of the garden are two one-off trees: 'the tree of life' and 'the tree of knowing right from wrong'.

street wise

What do you say about a tree? The lungs of the planet. Plants as tall as a house. Outbreaks of greenness in the heart of the grey city. What do you say about a tree? Decades in growing. Dying each winter, to be born again.

Great stuff, wood. You can make it into chairs and tables. You can make it into floors and roofs. You can even make it into a cross.

Something grows. Huge. Slow. Giving us shelter, giving us oxygen. And we cut it down and make it into something to nail someone on to.

What do you say about a tree? Use it for good. Let it breathe for us. Or chainsaw it with selfishness and carve it into a club to beat people around the head. Trees remind us of that one tree: the knowledge of good and evil. Which do you know most about?

Genesis 3:7; Exodus 3:2; Deuteronomy 21:23; 1 Kings 19:4; Psalm 96:12; Isaiah 55:12; Ezekiel 47:12; Matthew 27:5; Mark 14:32; Jude 12; Revelation 22:2

sign posts

Acts of creation are ordinarily reserved for gods and poets, but humbler folk may circumvent this restriction if they know how. To plant a pine, for example, one need be neither god nor poet; one need only own a good shovel. *–Aldo Leopold.*

Keep a green tree in your heart and perhaps a singing bird will come. *–Chinese proverb*

For in the true nature of things, if we rightly consider, every green tree is far more glorious than if it were made of gold and silver. *–Martin Luther*

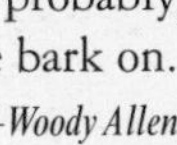

As the poet said, 'only God can make a tree', probably because it's so hard to figure out how to get the bark on.
–Woody Allen

Look at a leaf. Just think about it for a bit.

What tree has God told *you* not to eat from?

Check your choices. Which direction is good? Which is evil?

Don't chuck your old Christmas tree on the neighbour's skip, plant the thing.*

Plant a tree. Plant lots of trees. Plant a forest.

Choose a tree in your garden (or plant one). Every time you look at it, let it be a symbol. Use it to remind you to choose God's way.

way out!

'Go on, take a bite, nothing will change . . .' Who said that before?

Do what you want. It's your life.

Cut all the trees down in your garden, so you can work on your tan – the summers are warming up.

'O Lord, *argh!* . . . Amen!'

*Unless it's plastic.

Gridlock

street life

Things to do, people to see, stuff to buy, places to be. And here I am stuck in the traffic jam from hell. The great equalizer: Robin Reliants going the same speed as Mercs. This is going to put me behind all day. Hate it when I'm chasing my 'to do' list. Phone ahead. Let them know I'll be late. No signal. Great. I can write some notes . . . where's my file? Where's my pen? No pen! Wait, I've got a signal now. Ring through my ETA. Come on, pick up. 'Yes, hi. Look, I'm stuck in . . . hello?' Low battery! Argh!

street bible 2 Corinthians 11:23b-30; 12:9b-10

I've done more! Worked harder, been locked up more, had more punishment beatings, faced death so often we're on first-name terms! Let's compare scars: five lots of thirty-nine lashes, three lots of rod whackings, one time almost stoned to death, three times shipwrecked – including forty-eight hours in the open sea. I've lived out of a suitcase. My life's been like a blockbuster: white-water rivers, gangland muggings, race hate from non-Jews, race hate from Jews, treble jeopardy – in the city, in the country, at sea . . . Who reckons they're weak? I'll tell them about weak. Who reckons they're being sucked down, on the verge of really messing up? Sometimes it feels like I'm burning up.

If I'm going to brag, I'll brag about the stuff that shows my weak side.

So now I love bragging about my lack of energy, my weakness – 'cos then the Liberator's power really kicks in. And it's doing his reputation the world of good, so I'm over the moon about all the things that make me weak: the slurs, the hassles, the victimization, the problems. For when I've no energy of my own, it's bizarre, but that's when I'm at my strongest.

street wise

We live in a rush-hour society. Well, it was just a rush hour. Now it's 24/7 gridlock out there. And it's not just cars. We're stuck in gridlocked lives, jammed in, stressed out, unable to move for the traffic of everyday existence.

So take a turning off the highway once in a while. Wander the back roads of life for a bit. Try to schedule a day when you don't have to do so much. And try to live out the Sabbath idea. When God asked us to put a day aside, it wasn't so we could attend three Sunday services, a youth group meeting and redecorate the hall. It was so we could worship and rest.

Psalm 1, 23:1–3, 46:10; Ecclesiastes 3:2–8; Matthew 11:28–30; Philippians 4:4–7; Romans 5:4, 5

sign posts

There is time for everything. *–Thomas Edison*

The time to relax is when you don't have time for it. *–Sidney J. Harris*

The bad news is time flies. The good news is you're the pilot. *–Michael Althsuler*

I have noticed that the people who are late are often so much jollier than the people who have to wait for them. *–E. V. Lucas*

what if?

Do you feel like you have enough time in your life?

What if you walked instead of taking the car?

Are you always late for trains, meetings, etc.? What could you do about it?

Does the pressure of time make you angry?

What would you do if you had more hours in the day?

If we gave you a gift of two hours now, what would you spend it on?

straight ahead

Next time you're in a traffic jam pass the person in the next car a jelly baby.

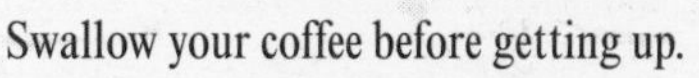

Swallow your coffee before getting up.

Make an appointment in your diary to meet 'Mr Space and Ms Reflection'. Make sure you attend the meeting.

Learn how to say 'no'. Just because someone asks you to do something or attend something doesn't mean you always have to do it.

way out!

Rev your engine as hard as you can. It soon speeds things up.

Take it out on a close friend/partner.

Just say 'yes' to everything.

Realize God took the seventh day off but said nothing about having to take a lunch hour.

'O Lord, *nothing* . . . Amen!'

cROWd

street life

Thirty thousand people, chanting: 'There's only one Wayne Rooney, one Wayne Rooney.' It's a group thing: you never hear a lone voice contradicting . . .

'Actually, that's not true!' says the lone voice.

The crowd come back in unison, 'Oh really? Tell me more, tell me more, if you think you're hard enough.'

'Well, a different Wayne Rooney lives at no. 38 down my street, so you're not singing any more! You're not singing any more!'

Wouldn't it be great to get a bit of social conscience to replace the idolization of celebrities? Football stadia ringing with the sound of the fans of the poor shouting, 'We'll support you evermore.' Or fans of both teams rattling the rafters with 'We love you, parents, we do.' But that'd involve someone having the guts to start something new and not just follow the crowd. Rare.

street bible

Ephesians 4:17-24

So, I'm being straight with you, straight from the Boss – stand out from the crowd; don't be like the rest of them drifting through life like nothing matters. They're groping round in the dark. They blocked off God's life source and can't quite suss what it's all about, can't quite click 'open' on their deep places, everything just freezes. So 'right and wrong' means nothing to them. They do whatever they fancy, have whatever they fancy . . .

But you stand out: you're different: you were coached in the Liberator lifestyle. You've taken it in; you've taken it on; you're convinced by it – it's about debagging the old you, your dark side, your 'former life', which just twists you up with cravings. Then what? You just stay naked? No, God's Spirit advises you and you get kitted out in the new you, your vibrant side, your 'new life' – tailor-made for you. You put it on and start looking more and more like God, unpolluted and doing the right thing.

street wise

The truth is that most of the time we don't really think about things. We swallow the myths, believe the hype. Being a Christian means swimming against the tide; it means looking at the accepted behaviour of the world and making our own minds up in the light of Christ as to which direction to follow.

Exodus 23:2; Matthew 9:36; Romans 12:1–2; Revelation 7:9, 19:1

sign posts

Most people are other people. Their thoughts are someone else's opinions, their lives a mimicry, their passions a quotation. *–Oscar Wilde*

We would worry less about what others think of us if we realized how seldom they do. *–Ethel Barrett*

We would know mankind better if we were not so anxious to resemble one another. *–Johann Wolfgang von Goethe*

We should not conform with human traditions to the extent of setting aside the command of God. *–St Basil*

what if?

In what ways do you conform to the world around you?

Are there things you do because 'everyone does it'?

What if the crowd's right?

straight ahead

Go to a train station at rush hour. Walk in the opposite direction to the crowd. Notice how hard it is.

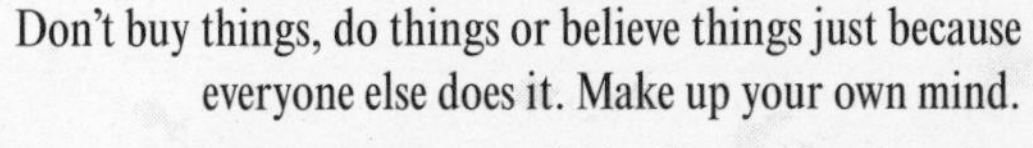

Don't buy things, do things or believe things just because everyone else does it. Make up your own mind.

Create your own mission statement. Write down the values that shape your behaviour, the priorities you have as an individual, the way that you intend to behave. Keep it safe and refer to it frequently.

Contrary to popular belief, lemmings do not follow the crowd, nor do they jump into lakes in a form of rodent suicide pack. So stand up for lemmings. The next time someone talks about lemmings jumping off a cliff, shout, 'No! You are being a lemming-ist, and I wish to challenge you with the facts.'

Find out what everyone else would do to get out of doing this. Then just do the same.

'O Lord, *halle-flippin-lujah* . . . Amen!'

Noise

street life

Need to remix the soundtrack to my day. Got at least forty-eight channels on my mental mixing desk and most of them are just nudging up past the Annoying level. Wish the Great Sound Engineer in the sky would pull the dial down on cars, lorries, buses, trains, roadworks, building works, sirens, car alarms, car stereos, mobile phones. Maybe he could sample a trickling brook or two, paste that into the mix. Take an ambient mic into the woods, that'd change the atmos. Or a quality digital recording of some thoughtful silence – hey, a CD of that! Now we're talking, or not . . . preferably.

street bible

Psalm 46:10

> 'Shut up . . . Shut off . . . Shut out . . . and
> In the silence . . . (x 3) sense God: connect!
> He says, 'For I'll be profiled and praised, the world will be amazed;
> I'll be known and named, shown and famed.
> My name will be large, lifted, enflamed!
> So shut up . . . Shut off . . . Shut out . . . and
> In the silence . . . connect!' (x 4 to fade)

street wise

In years gone by they used to torture people with noise. Put a prisoner in the cell and batter him with noise to keep him from sleeping, and pretty soon his spirit will have broken and he'll tell you anything you need to know.

Sometimes it seems as though our lives are being subjected to the same treatment. We live in a volume-up society. Everywhere you go there is noise: it wears us down, stopping us from concentrating on what really matters, diverting us to other, more superficial concerns. Noise brings stress; noise brings anxiety; noise wears us out.

And here's the point: it's hard to hear God speaking to you if you're always listening to something else. It's hard to hear the still small voice if you won't switch off the earthquake. We all need to listen to God; we all need a bit of quiet to recharge our batteries. But we can't recharge our batteries if we won't stop moving. So, give yourself a break. Press the pause button on your life. Turn off the TV. Unplug the stereo. Switch off the MP3s, CDs, tapes, mobile phones, DVDs . . . Plug into God and recharge the batteries of your life.

1 Kings 19:9–18; Job 3:26; Psalm 23:2; Proverbs 17:1; Isaiah 9:6, 26:3; Zephaniah 3:17; John 14:27; Colossians 3:15; Philippians 4:7

sign posts

We have noisy hearts.
–Richard Foster

'Rest in the Lord; wait patiently for him.' In Hebrew, 'Be silent to God and let him mould you.' Keep still and he will mould you to the right shape.
–Martin Luther

With silence one irritates the Devil.
*–Bulgarian proverb**

All the troubles of life come upon us because we refuse to sit quietly for a while each day in our rooms.
–Blaise Pascal

what if?

What if you really had a quiet time each day?

What if there was a five-minute silence in a church service?

We're always listening: aren't there four other senses as well?

straight ahead

Sit quietly for five minutes. Don't do anything. Don't listen to anything. Don't watch anything. Just sit. See if you can make it.

Try driving to work without the car stereo on.

way out!

Turn the volume up so you can't hear other people banging the walls.

Always have the TV on in the background . . . for company.

Go on a silent retreat.

Turn off the TV. You won't generate the next big idea while half-listening to *Stenders*. Ideas are shy.

'O Lord, *pardon?*. . . Amen!'

*No, really. Bulgarians need proverbs too, you know.

NeedLe

street life

Just one needle – in a clinic, fine, but abandoned under a tree in a public park, freaky! I stare at it: is there some disease sniggering away, waiting to pounce? Wish I could analyse the DNA of the user, track them down and give them a good slapping. What if I picked it up, would I catch something? What if my toddler had found it? What if he'd played with it?

What if I wasn't so 'me, me, me' about the whole thing? What if I stopped to consider the person at the sharp end? What if I could do something to stop people needing drugs? What if I had a high, way better than anything drug-induced, to offer people? What if I'd been keeping that to myself?

street bible

2 Timothy 3:1-4

Don't say I didn't warn you: before it all gets wrapped up there'll be some ugly stuff flying round. People will have multiple love affairs – with themselves, with money. They'll be cocky, arrogant, mouthy. They'll ignore their parents. 'Thanks' won't be in their vocab. They'll fit in with the rest of the polluted hate-culture. They'll only bother to talk if it's malicious. They'll only get off their backsides for a good scrap. Good things give them the creeps; they jump ship when it suits them; they do whatever when it suits them and they're so full of themselves they can't take any criticism on board. They'll love the next high more than God.

street wise

If life is flat then you have to find your highs somewhere – in music, dancing, sport, bungee jumping. Some go to darker places. Their highs come through the neck of a bottle, or down the needle of a syringe. Of course, it's not getting high that's the problem: it's coming down. And the daring stuff that everyone warns you of, the ones that promise you so much – those are the killers. Literally.

So what do we do? First, make sure our own highs are the real thing. Find joy in God and we're less likely to search for it elsewhere. Get high on holiness and a lift from love – the only addictive substance that actually does you good.

Second, look beyond the addicts to their lives. What can we do for people with lives so empty they rely on alcohol or drugs? What challenge can we be to those who think they can't get high on anything other than their own pleasures? Have we really shown them a different way? Or have we given up on them?

streetlights

2 Kings 7:3–9; Psalm 104:15; Proverbs 20:1, 23:20, 23:31, 31:6; Song of Songs 1:2; Isaiah 55:1; Matthew 9:17; John 2:3; 1 Corinthians 3:16, 6:19, 20; 1 Timothy 5:23; Titus 2:1–15; Jude 8; Revelation 16:19

signposts

The basic thing nobody asks is why do people take drugs of any sort? Why do we have these accessories to normal living to live? I mean, is there something wrong with society that's making us so pressurized that we cannot live without guarding ourselves against it?

–John Lennon

The answers to life's problems aren't at the bottom of a beer bottle, they're on TV.

–Homer Simpson

what if?

Where do you get your 'highs'?

Why should Christians avoid drugs: (a) because they're addictive? (b) because they're harmful? (c) because they're illegal? (d) all three?

Why do you think people take drugs?

Are you a recovering -aholic?*

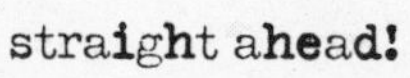

straight ahead!

Just say 'no'.†

Support and pray for people who are working with drug addicts and those recovering from addiction.

way out!

Ignore this and there will be no way out.

'O Lord, *you!* . . . Amen!'

*'Work', 'TV', 'sex' or other. †Or 'no, thank you', if you prefer.

Modern Celtic Blessing

May your bed and your computer be bug free
May your software never crash
May all your debts be from generous acts
May all your mistakes be from your freedom to fail
May your spillages be from having too much fun
May you only stub your toe on something you'd lost
May you only get a flat tyre when you're opposite a garage
. . . that's open
. . . that does tyres
. . . that fit.
May all your spots be from fat-free chocolate
May all your blotches be from love bites – which you can hide
May all your illnesses bring you reflection and insight
May all your worries make you pray
May God calm you, disarm you
Then fight all your battles for you
And may you know
Really know
That the God of grace is for you.
Amen.